SAVE US FROM OURSELVES

Open Letter to the Earthmen on the Transformation of a Misguided World to Love, Peace and Justice

By :

IYKE NATHAN UZORMA

Harbinger of the Last Covenant

CHRIST RESTORATION CENTER

CONTACTS:

Authorunit
17130 Van Buren Blvd, Ste 238, Riverside, CA 92504
+1, 877-826-5888
www.authorunitcom

Dr. Moses Ayuketa,
1766 E. 61st Street, Tulsa, Ok 74136
+1, 9188498130
ayuketamoses@gmail.com

Archbishop (Prof.) Iyke Nathan U.,
P. O. Box 1562, Effurun, Warri, Nigeria;
Phone +234-807-563-7746,
WhatsApp +234-818-379-6658;
Email: harbingeroffice@gmail.com;
www.iykenathanuzorma.org

CONTENTS

"I write this letter in full recognition that it is for the good of our world; for the over all well being and embellishment of the earthmen in divine terms. I write this letter in the consciousness that we, the entire children of men, belong to one human family. I speak in this material to those who believe in God and those who do not. I speak to those who hold that science will possibly solve all human problems and those who do not. I speak to the entire children of men of what we must do to enhance, individually and collectively, the practical aspects of Love, Peace and Justice in our world. I want all humans to know that it may be difficult, but not impossible, to achieve true Love, Peace and Justice.

— HARBINGER OF THE LAST COVENANT.

All glories to the **One Eternal Almighty God** for the ability given to me by His Divine Spirit to write and present this treatise to the children of men.

I sincerely appreciate the encouragement of my queen, Lady Dr. Imaobong Udeme Uzorma, in the formation of this material. In the same vein, I deeply appreciate the efforts of Dr. Francis Okezie, Prince Jacob Esin and James Simon, for the publication and spread of this work.

The 'Harbinger Media Team', especially Dr. Livingstone Amos, Engr. Segun Arise, Hon. Nora Kingsley, Mrs. Proze Efeise and Mrs. Maro Lucky, are all appreciated for their organizing assistance in the formation of this material. And for proof-reading of the manuscript, I appreciate my following lovely ones: Helen Nwoye, Promise Uzorma, Chukwuka Uzorma, Nelson Alabi, Hilary Okolie, Anita Okotete and Caleb Unyah.

My lovely friends, especially Kofi Panford, Dr. Ese Ahalonu and Frank Fiaka, including my coordinators in different countries, as well as all my lovely partners worldwide, are all deeply appreciated for standing by the mission of the Harbinger of the Last Covenant. God bless you all.

Iyke Nathan Uzorma
Harbinger of the Last Covenant

Some Comments On The Works Of The Author

"It is indeed a miracle that Prof. Iyke Nathan Uzorma, a well known Guru and Perfect Master of Esoteric Mysteries, has been humbled and convicted by the Holy Spirit to acknowledge and accept the sovereignty of the true Christ over his life."
--- PROF. OLADEJO OKEDIJI Former Dean, Faculty of Social Sciences; University of Lagos, Nigeria.

*****

"Though several publications on religious and spiritual matters exist, but from my personal experience, none the world over is as authoritative as the works of Prof. Iyke Nathan Uzorma, Harbinger of the Last Covenant."
--- His Excellency, YURI KWAKU BAAWINE Former Ambassador of Ghana to Saudi Arabia.

*****

"My meeting Prof. lyke Nathan Uzorma, Harbinger of the Last Covenant, in Nigeria, greatly lifted my spirit and opened my eyes more on deeper aspects of the mysteries of life."
--- PROF. YOSIAH MAGEMBE BWATWA Dean, Faculty of Education, Tumaini University, Dar-es-Salaam, Tanzania.

*****

"My respected mentor, Prof. Iyke Nathan Uzorma, Harbinger of the Last Covenant, thanks for teaching me the reality of the forces of darkness, their manipulations and weaknesses. Thank you sir and May God continue to use you to bless our generation."
--- DR. MOSES AYUKETA Presiding Bishop, Christ Restoration Centre, Tulsa, Okl., USA.

*****

"We thank the Almighty God for giving us His 'Harbinger of the Last Covenant', to open our eyes and bring true spiritual awakening in our time"
---His Royal Majesty PROF. AMUZIENWA

DELE ODIGBO, Ezeigwe 43rd of Nkwesi kingdom, Oguta, Imo State, Nigeria

*****

"The books of Prof. Iyke Nathan Uzorma, Harbinger of the Last Covenant, are nobel and highly enriching to humanity."
--- PROF. SMART O. NWAOKORO
University of Benin, Nigeria.

*****

"When great Souls speak, mysteries are demystified, but when the Harbinger of the Last Covenant speaks, great Souls learn wisdom to teach others".
--- PASTOR GABRIEL S. OBICHUKWU
Redeemed Christian Church of God, Abakaliki, Nigeria.

*****

PREFACE

By The 'Harbinger Media Team'

This publication, **'SAVE US FROM OURSELVES'**, is an open letter written to mankind by the **'Harbinger of the Last Covenant'**, His Grace, Archbishop (Prof.) Iyke Nathan Uzorma. It is intended for a practical solution to the current state of violence and wicked practices in our world. We, the 'Harbinger Media Team', are strongly of the opinion that this letter is a practical contribution towards the transformation of the misguided world to love, peace and justice. Therefore, we hope that it will respond in no small measure to the acute need of our time.

As you peruse this letter, you will discover that it is not just a mere letter, but a highly advanced divine lecture that proposes practical solutions to terrorism, corruption, dehumanization and all forms of wickedness in our world, by the knowledge and application of the immutable

Universal Laws exposed here. You may also see this letter as a peaceful co-existence renaissance handbook, written from a perspective that, if fully comprehended and applied, will serve as a panacea to all that have risen from ourselves against ourselves on Earth.

Over the years, efforts have been made by governments, institutions and highly respected and concerned people to bring about peace and peaceful co-existence in the world. These efforts include but not limited to preaching peace, writing books on peace and peaceful co-existence, sending diplomats to peace keeping missions in times of crisis, integrating peace studies in some of our institutions of higher learning, setting up peace advocacy groups, putting up enormous efforts to combat terrorism, amongst others. But conversely these enormous efforts have not succeeded in enthroning the desired peace on Earth.

The author of this letter, **'Harbinger of the Last Covenant'**, needs no introduction to some people in different parts of the world. Many people have testified that he is indeed a blessing to mankind. He rose from the peak of darkness to the Light of God. He is a man of deep knowledge and mysteries. The Spirit of God has used him to establish testimonies in the lives of people from different parts of the world, including raising the dead in some occasions.

His Grace, Archbishop (Prof) Iyke Nathan Uzorma, is the author of several books. Some of his books contain information coming to this world for the first time. These include Hidden Truth of Man and Woman, Verses of Eternal Truth, Deeper Realities of Existence, 7 Cycles of Astral Attacks on Money and How to Overcome, Hidden Terrorists, Secrets From Heaven, My <u>300</u> Minutes Experience of Heaven, Occult Grandmaster Now in Christ, etc. More of his deep spiritual expositions are contained in 'Prof. Iyke Nathan Uzorma' YouTube Channel and Facebook Page. When we (the Harbinger Media Team) asked the author to summarise this 'open letter to the earthmen', he said:

> *"This letter is designed to save us from ourselves. I t provides practical guidance on how to defeat all that we have set in motion to subjugate us.*

"It is written for the entire children of men in the light of one family of humanity. If we humans, individually and collectively, put into practice the message of this treatise, we will initiate a new beginning in the formation of a world of sanity. This letter holds the possibility of achieving this, in the consciousness of brotherhood of all existences.

"This book also provides a glimpse into the actions of the Forces of Light and the forces of darkness in the realms beyond, in the light of divine intervention for the world of man or human subjugation, amongst other important things.

"The conclusion of this material gives a strong warning to the Earth-world, related to a coming global catastrophe that will dwarf the COVID-19 Pandemic.

"This letter is for all the children of men, regardless of religion,

race, nationality, tradition and belief systems. The time to act on salvaging our world is now".

The reader will observe that this letter is written from a universal perspective, irrespective of our differing religions, beliefs and apparent human differences; the primary focus is human beings. Furthermore, this open letter x-rays how the energies of our negative thought-patterns contribute to what the author calls the 'universal pool of probabilities', from which the impetus of relevant wicked acts on Earth is derived. It also explains how this impedes peaceful co-existence. This letter shows how we can contribute our energy daily to the sanity of our world in love, for the realization of lasting peace and justice.

The contributions of great sages and extra-terrestrial intelligences towards the realization of peace and justice is also elaborated and simplified in this open letter, for greater understanding of all and sundry. And the words spoken by the

Lord in this regard, at diverse times and places, are not left out in this book.

The author says that: **"we have fully entered the era of planetary winnowing and this is the most dangerous hour for anyone to uphold a vicious mental pattern"**. And in the words of our friend, Dr. Francis Okezie, Abuja, Nigeria, who read the manuscript:

> ***"This book captures the essence of the teachings in all holy books ever written, explaining the deeper realities of the various energies discharged by our thoughts, words and actions. It also clearly shows the practical pathway to save our world from the imminent catastrophe awaiting man at this end-time"***.

In addition to this open letter, the author made annotation on each page of the letter, for the guidance of the reader. When we asked him about the possibility of man upholding the true essence of this message, he said: **"The spider says he has inside his belly sufficient materials for building his own house"**. Again, we talked to him concerning the present depraved situation of human beings, and he responded thus: **"Remember, if you want to befriend the pig you must be prepared to meddle in the mud"**. On whether the people of this world, from different religious backgrounds, will accept this letter, the author said: **"It is not what you are called that matters but what you answer to"**.

The solution that the **Harbinger of the Last Covenant** has proffered in this book, for the transformation of the misguided world to love, peace and justice, and the realization of lasting peace on Earth, should be taken seriously. The Harbinger Media Team is glad to be associated with the noble objectives of this 'open letter to the earthmen', with the hope that it will fulfill the good intentions of the **Harbinger of the Last Covenant** to our world.

May the reader of this book be blessed.

Dr. Livingstone Amos
Head, Harbinger Media Team

TRANSFORMING A MISGUIDED WORLD

Dear earthmen – sons and daughters of men in the world of man – whether you are in Nigeria, United Kingdom, United States, India, Ghana, South Africa, Kenya, Canada, Afghanistan,

Iraq, Syria, Russia, China, Philippines, Saudi Arabia, Brazil, Australia, Egypt, Libya, Cameroon, Spain, Jamaica or Japan: anywhere you are on the Earth surface reading this material, I wish you Peace flowing from the Throne of the Almighty God of Creation, even His Spirit of Life which abides within you, gives you life, and within which you abide. Amen.

The subject matter of this my open letter to the people of our world, entitled **'Save Us From Ourselves'**, deals on the transformation of a misguided world to Love, Peace and Justice. This is designed towards the practical realization of genuine Peace on Earth.

In the recognition and realization of brotherhood of all nations, all humans, all existences, I present this work to the earthmen. In the quest for sustainable Peace in our world, this treatise, in my understanding, is a serious practical, psychological and spiritual framework in our sincere attempt to provide the way forward with lasting solutions.

ANNOTATION:
Man must be saved from himself; he must be saved from the existence in the mode of darkness.

Dear friend and reader of this letter, in the light of the prevailing mass killings hitherto on the surface of Earth, arising from man against man – from ourselves against ourselves – including the COVID-19 Pandemic and other related mass predicaments, I give you this treatise. I urge you, dear reader, to seriously consider the core essence of this treatise, which I sincerely believe is needed now for true solutions to the unpleasant situations in our world.

For instance, my nation, Nigeria, from whence I write this letter, is currently embroiled in terrorism, kidnapping, threats of secession, ravaging bandits, destruction of property, amongst other manifestations inimical to the existence of sanity in Light, namely, peaceful co-existence of humans. We can live in Peace when we truly commit ourselves to it; we can make it.

ANNOTATION:
We have to kill hate before it kills us; a tree that does not know how to dance will be taught by the winds.

THE VICIOUS CYCLE OF KILLINGS

The earthman must be warned in this era of the dire consequences of sticking to the path of shedding human blood. Earthmen, refrain yourselves from hate, live in love, follow the path of peaceful dialogue for the sake of Peace and do not rush into war – the enclave of battles and killings – in your families, communities, regions, and nations. Remember, war is death. And I tell you: war doesn't determine who is right or wrong, rather it determines who is alive, maimed or dead. Let us, the children of men, give Love, Peace and Justice the chance to triumph in our midst.

ANNOTATION:
Let's give peace the chance to grow, it's for our collective good in the world of man.

Even when you score so-called 'victory' in war by maiming and killing other humans, unknown to you, you entangle yourself in the cosmic web of 'karmic' burden, in the cycle of endless killings. This is strictly in accordance with the Universal Law of Reciprocal Action, which is immutable. By this, killing your fellow men, is transposed into 'you' being killed someday in the journey of life, via a cosmological verdict. The Great Lord Jesus the Christ and Saint John spoke of this thus:

> ***"Then said Jesus unto him, Put up again thy sword into his place: for all they that take the sword shall perish with the sword"*** (Math. 26:52; KJV).

> ***"He that leadeth into captivity shall go into captivity: he that killeth with the*** sword **must be killed with the sword** *"* (Rev. 13:10; KJV).

ANNOTATION:
The Universal Law of Reciprocal Action must exert itself in all facets of being.

The earthmen, in general terms, are ignorant of the workings of the Universal Law of Reciprocal Action. They do not know that when you kill a person in one way or another, you will surely be killed likewise someday in the journey of life. The journey of life itself is equally not well understood. Some earthmen look at it solely from one appearance of the earth- life, but it is more than that.

Consequently, some people think: 'Oh, look at this man; he killed fellow earthmen but finally died a peaceful death; he wasn't killed by anyone'. Thus, they think it doesn't really follow that, he who kills with the sword must die by the sword. They do not know that man is a Soul (spirit-essence), embedded in the camouflage systems of the material body, and that the Soul is a prime identity encapsulated in multitudinous and multidimensional rudiments of motion.

ANNOTATION:

If you drink poison, thinking that it is a fruit juice, the poison will work as poison; ignorance is no excuse.

The earthman isn't aware in general terms that the Soul, which he is, is a gestalt of multifarious appearances and realities, in which experiences are gathered beyond time and space. Therefore, the Soul is in a constant state of electromagnetic flux, within the ambit of the Universal Law of Soul Transmigration.

Furthermore, the earthman is not aware that the Soul is divinely configured to wear different bodies in manifestations. They are oblivious of the fact that this reality operates strictly under the Universal Law of Soul Transmigration, to the end that we reap what we sow, via the Universal Law of Reciprocal Action. This is regardless of the period of time enacted between the moment of action and the moment of reaping the fruit thereof. Saint Paul wrote thus:

ANNOTATION:
You are a Soul. In certain higher divine terms, the Soul is not what you have, but what you are.

"Be not deceived; God is not mocked: for whatsoever a man soweth, that shall he also reap" *(Gal. 6:7; KJV).*

Now, for instance, recall the case of the biblical Prophet Elijah. It will possibly give you a clue about how the Universal Law of Reciprocal Action works, in conjunction with the Universal Law of Soul Transmigration. These Universal Laws, and all the Universal Laws in the Universes of God, are immutable – inexorable – being the unchangeable Will of the Almighty God in motion.

Now, Elijah murdered about 450 earthmen in his time, who were considered then in certain terms to be 'false prophets'. (See 1 Kings 18). Nevertheless, whatever reason you have for killing a person, including but not limited to the

ANNOTATION:
We are now in the era of the Last Covenant, the era of love and peace, not the era of hurting and killing people. Let us cue into the spirit of this era.

claim that you were commanded by God to do so, will not exonerate you from being killed someday. There was a day that the Lord appeared to me and said, amongst other things:

> ***"If I tell the earthman to do a thing to another man; a thing which he wouldn't want to be done to himself: as he carries it out in the happiness of obeying Me, behold, he will surely receive the punishment thereof, for not pleading for My mercy to the other person".***

After that one cycle experience of the earth-life, in which he killed some children of men – "**And Elijah said unto them, Take the prophets of Baal; let not one of them escape. And they took them: and Elijah brought them down to**

ANNOTATION:
The Spirit of God still speaks as it was in the beginning, especially to those who have ears to hear.

the brook Kishon, and slew them there" (1 Kings 18:25; KJV) – what followed him (Elijah) later in the journey of life? To begin with, a stage was set for him (Elijah) to return again to the physical realms of Earth. Thus, it was said by God: **"Behold, I will send you Elijah the prophet before the coming of the great and dreadful day of the LORD"** (Mal. 4:5; KJV).

At last, Elijah finally returned, via the Universal Law of Soul Transmigration, as John the Baptist. The Disciples of Christ, who didn't know initially that John the Baptist was the returned Elijah, asked the Lord for clarification, because it was said that Elijah will come first before Christ.

The Disciples believed in the Lord Jesus as the expected Christ. However, they wondered whether the Scriptures were void in stating that Elijah will come first before Christ. (See Math.

ANNOTATION:
Now, you are far more than the physical aspect of being that you know as yourself.
Remember, John the Baptist was Elijah. Who and what are you?

17:10). To set the Scripture in the proper perspective, in the light of eternal truth, the Great Lord Jesus the Christ told them:

> ***"Elijah truly shall first come, and restore all things. But I say unto you, that Elijah is come already, and they knew him not, but have done unto him whatsoever they listed. Likewise shall also the Son of man suffer of them"(Math. 17:11,12; KJV).***

Consequently, the Disciples got Him right. They recognised that He spoke specifically about John the Baptist as the returned Elijah. **"Then the disciples understood that He spake unto them of John the Baptist"** (Math. 17:13; KJV). In this divine terms, therefore, it is clear that Elijah returned to the Earth-world and was born as John the Baptist. This is in the

ANNOTATION:
The spiritual essence of the Holy Scriptures transcends the mundane interpretation generally given within organised religions.

light of the continuity of the journey of life, as related to every human, in accordance to the Universal Law of Soul Transmigration.

Elijah came back as John the Baptist. As John the Baptist, he did many things to the glory of God, including revealing the divine identity of Jesus as the expected Christ. However, when it came to the point of his departure from the physical realms of Earth (death in human terms), how did that go? How was his death enacted? He was killed by the sword. **"And immediately the king sent an executioner, and commanded his head to be brought: and he went and beheaded him in the prison"** (Mark 6:27; KJV).

As Elijah, he killed with the sword; and as John the Baptist, he was killed with the sword. This fulfilled a fundamental Universal Law of Reciprocal Action, which the Lord Himself

ANNOTATION:
Whosoever kills must eventually be killed in the journey of life.
This is by virtue of the immutable Universal Law, which is inexorable.

referred to when He said: **"For all they that take the sword shall perish with the sword"**. This should serve as a great lesson to the present generation of the children of men. We must return to the path of Peace, Love and Justice in mercy to all, so as to subjugate the cycle of endless killings.

A MESSAGE TO ALL

We, the earthmen, can't continue on the path of wickedness and expect to make true progress in the right essence of the journey of life. No nation makes true progress in the journey of life whilst dwelling on the path of dichotomy, killings and destruction. We must change and revert to the path of Love, Peace and Justice. We must begin by seeing ourselves in oneness of the human family, regardless of tribe, race, religion, political party and other divisive tendencies. Herein lies the core essence of this letter.

ANNOTATION:
Hate, killings and maiming dwarfs the progress of life, individually and collectively.

Now, dear reader, be informed from the onset of this letter that I do not present this treatise to the children of men solely under the ambit of one particular earthly organisation, be it physical, social, religious or metaphysical. I am not speaking here to the earthmen based upon the platform of any particular so-called superior organized religious denomination on Earth, in this case, under the presumptuous cum outright delusion of religious supremacy and superiority.

Thus, this letter, **'save us from ourselves'**, is based on the related divine knowledge directly granted to the **Harbinger of the Last Covenant** from 'above'. Now, the word 'above' is in connection with dimensions and realms of Divine Light existing beyond the physical systems of reality generally known. I mean the realms of Eternal Light more valid and vivid than the physical world that we know; the realms of Light that are truly committed to the guidance of the earthmen in Light – Love, Peace and Justice.

To this end, I have come to comprehend in this my earth-life, in the light of eternal truth, existence and true nature of reality, that for Love, Peace and Justice to have dominion in our lives, individually and collectively, we – the children of men – must be saved from ourselves. Therefore, dear reader, I am addressing this material to you – to the entire children of men – solely from the platform of divine reality, irrespective of belief systems and other mundane considerations.

In certain terms, however, this publication may be seen as a little drop of water contributed into the big ocean encapsulating the path of peaceful co-existence of the human family. I say this, for instance, when this material is compared to the big plans of the government of diverse nations towards achieving Peace on Earth. However,

ANNOTATION:
The earthman can only be salvaged from the platform of divine reality, not from the mundane systems.

it is said that **'small deeds done are better than great deeds planned'.** The 'small deeds,' which this material may represent, will hopefully bear great fruits in the world of man.

As you take time to ascertain the authenticity of the above statement, via this material, I pray that we, individually and collectively, be firmly situated on the path of Divine Love, Peace and Justice, for the wellbeing of the human family. This requires a change in our innermost consciousness, as the slogan goes in my country, Nigeria, **"change begins with me"**. This is true.

RECOGNITION OF ONENESS

I write this letter in full recognition that it is for the good of our world; for the overall wellbeing and embellishment of the earthmen in divine terms. I write this letter in the consciousness

ANNOTATION:
Contribute your quota towards love, peace and justice in mercy for all.
The big tree of today was once a small seed.

that we, the entire children of men, belong to one human family. This is one of the greatest lessons I have learned in my earth-life.

I have learned that we have to be our brother's keeper at all times, if we must be situated and sustained on the path of divine ascent in the journey of life. We must uphold Love and Justice for our individual Peace and the Peace of all humans – Peace of the earthmen. And until we, the children of men, uphold the path of this recognition in Love, we may not subjugate the things that hold us down in the mundane dungeons of wickedness, from which we must be salvaged.

Nevertheless, the mind-set of this treatise is embedded with due consideration, and respect to diverse belief systems of the children of men, but towards the central goal of this material, namely, Love, Peace and Justice in our world. As I

ANNOTATION:
The lessons you learn in this life are more than the events that brought them up.
All changes will rise from within the consciousness.

communicate to you, the reader, via this material, I am aware that several sages, wise men, spiritual masters, religious heroes and prophets of old, from different parts of the world, in all the ages even in our time, have spoken along this line of spiritual guidance at diverse levels.

The diverse manifestations of the Lord in different parts of the world, at different levels of the One Eternal Spirit we call 'God', have also provided guidance for us, the children of men, on the path of Light and spiritual civilisation, based upon Divine Love and selfless service to humanity. But most times we have reciprocated with aspersions, falsehood embedded with the rigidity of mental speculations, ignorance and outright rejection.

Therefore, the problem is not lack of information or material to guide us on the path of divine ascent, via the recognition of Love, Peace and

ANNOTATION:

The wise learns by hearing; the fool learns from experience. A child who forsakes the counsel of the wise won't excel; the wise who fails to counsel the child won't excel.

Justice, but our inability to hear and put into action the bona-fide divine principles that will guide us and save us from ourselves. We cannot comprehend divine reality with the rigid limitations of mental speculations, because the message of divine reality is for those who have the ears to hear.

Through greed for mundane aggrandisement, we often form misguided religious belief systems, arising from our misinterpretation of the teachings of the Lord and the sayings of the wise men, sages, prophets and spiritual masters of old. An African adage has it that **'the whole of nature is too small for a greedy man'**. Another African wise sayings go thus:

> *"A greedy person who grabs at everything and puts into his pockets without scrutiny will one day pocket a snake .... Where greed and avarice thrive, crises brew"*.

ANNOTATION:
Misguided belief systems are impediments to spiritual excellence in divine Light.
Remember, the misguided beliefs of the Jews led them to murder the Great Lord Jesus the Christ.

Today in the world of man, we have many things and great doctrines both to preach and hear about our religions, but what about the heart of Love, Peace and Justice in mercy? What about being our brother's keeper? Is this not evidently lacking in many quarters even in highly proclaimed religious systems? Through greed, we, the children of men, have 'grabbed and pocketed poisonous snakes' that are terrorising our world in many ways. We now need to be saved from ourselves, from the individual and mass production of our wrong thinking, ignorance and wickedness.

MISGUIDED MIND-SETS

One night, as I was praying and meditating on issues concerning the world of man, my inner consciousness, within the framework of the

---

ANNOTATION:
Greed is one of the five destructive channels of the mind.
The rest are lust, anger, vanity and attachment to mundane things.

a 'message from above' geared towards the presentation of this open letter to the people of our world. As aforementioned, this letter is made to provide practical guidance, to the rulers and to the ruled, into the way forward in our quest for sustainable Love, Peace and Justice in the world of man.

I was elated in my mind to write this admonition, following the divine message given to me. I gladly accepted this assignment, in full recognition of the core essence of 'Love, Peace and Justice' for the sanity of existence, towards the overall wellbeing of the earthmen in diverse enclaves, families, regions, nations and the entire world of man. And as 'change begins with me', I expect each and every reader to understand the core essence of this material and put same into practical application for our overall good.

ANNOTATION:
We must be practical and sincerely committed to the vital issues of love, peace and justice in our families, communities, nations and our world at large.

This is because the absence of Love, Peace and Justice at any given moment in our midst is a catalyst to diverse predicaments. The scourge of terrorism in our world today, as well as corruption, kidnapping, rape, armed robbery, assassination, torture, arson, religious extremism, war, cultism, rebellion, tribalism, amongst others, are all embedded with lack of Love, Peace and Justice. These have thoroughly misguided the consciousness of the earthmen; these are huge problems for the peaceful co-existence of all humans.

To this end, I am perfectly on the same page in this treatise with all humans, as far as seeking for Love, Peace and Justice on Earth is concerned. Yes, I am on the same page with you on the foregoing subject matter, irrespective of your tribe, race, religion, nationality, amongst others.

ANNOTATION:
"Change begins with me" is a powerful slogan of the government of Nigeria.
Whatever that is repulsive to you and to human existence, play a part in changing it for good, even if it is a little part in your thinking.

Dear reader and listener, the issue of peaceful co-existence on Earth is the prime duty of all humans, irrespective of race, tribe, religion and nationality. Thus, this material speaks to the children of men, as earlier stated, in due consideration of diverse belief systems, whilst not rigidly limited to the reference point of my religion or belief system. And more than that, this letter takes us also beyond religions into the subtle aspects of the divine spheres of being, transcending the world of man.

Consequently, in the divine terms of reality, transcending the mundane aspects generally known, Love, Peace and Justice are imperative to human existence. These are categorized, not only as the bona-fide nectar of certainty of the consciousness of being on the physical realms of Earth, but also as the basis for the brotherhood

ANNOTATION:
By divisive tendencies peace eludes the children of men.
When we recognise that we are one, it will be easier for us to
uphold the consciousness of peaceful co-existence.

of all existences, in the entire Universal Systems. In these lie the prime foundation of the 'paradise' we seek, individually and collectively.

ANCIENT VOICE

We must know, at a certain stage of higher reality in the strata of existence, that we, the children of men, belong to 'one family of humanity'. This must be understood and appreciated. We are already aware that natural disasters, viruses and whatever happens on Earth, including terrorists attack, leading to the mass death of humans, do not discriminate on who to kill or keep alive.

When natural disasters occur, like the COVID-19 Pandemic, for instance, people die not on the basis of religions, tribes, nationalities or race, but simply as humans. The lesson there is clear: what happens to one relatively happens to all, because we are one family of humanity.

ANNOTATION:
The nectar of existence is love, wherein lies true peace of mind.
Life without peace is worthless.

That is how we, the children of men, are seen by denizens of higher Planetary Systems – humanoid and Intelligences existing far beyond the world of man.

Therefore, I present this material to you, sons and daughters of men, anywhere you are, from the reference point of one family of humanity. I write this treatise to the earthmen from one little corner of our world, with the inner recognition that I may be, possibly, speaking with an ancient voice to some earthmen of the world of man, especially to those who have the ears to hear.

OPEN YOUR THOUGHTS

I am writing this letter to our brothers and sisters of the Christendom, wherein I am, as well as our brothers and sisters of the Muslim community. Also, this treatise is to our brothers and sisters

ANNOTATION:
The ancient voice is also the voice of now, for as long as it guides the earthman to rise in divine Light, in the strata of existence.

of Buddhism, Hinduism, Judaism, the traditional religions, governments of diverse nations and the pagans.

I speak in this material to those who believe in God and those who do not. I speak to those who hold that Science will possibly solve all human problems and those who do not. I speak to the entire children of men of what we must do to enhance, individually and collectively, the practical aspects of Love, Peace and Justice in our world. I want all humans to know that it may be difficult, but not impossible, to achieve true Love, Peace and Justice in the world of man. That is what this my open letter is all about.

This letter, **'Save us from ourselves'**, also brings some of the things spoken of old by some elevated masterminds for our good in diverse sacred writings, which we may have forgotten to put into practice. Furthermore, I speak here reminding all the earthmen of the divine

ANNOTATION:
We are all brothers and sisters of the one planetary family of Earth,
whether or not we know it.

messages in our time and communications from higher Extraterrestrial Intelligences in Divine Light, who dwells far beyond the world of man, on the subject matter of this treatise.

Some of the things said by the Great God of the Universe Himself, to the children of men, in His multitudinous diverse manifestations throughout the ages, on the ultimate divine importance of Love, Peace and Justice, crowns this material with the Light of Heaven. Thus, what we must do henceforth, individually and collectively, for Peace and Justice, as well as Love, to have dominion over the Earth, is the core essence of the presentation of this my open letter to the Earth-world.

God bless the reader.

NO ONE BIRD CAN OWN THE SKY AND NO ONE FISH CAN SWIM ALL THE WATERS.

- The Harbinger

ANNOTATION:
Don't idle around saying, 'let the will of God be done'.
Act in the power of goodness and manifest the will of God -- the
Light of Heaven -- on Earth.

ENHANCING THE GOOD OF OUR WORLD

Dear people of our Planet Earth, especially the reader of this material, as generally known, Love, Peace and Justice build the fabrics of human existence. These must be encapsulated in deep

ANNOTATION:
It is only from the divine platform that peace and love will flourish
in our midst.

mercy for fellow man and every creature; so that, by the Universal Law of Reciprocal Action, you will equally receive mercy in the hour of your needs.

The practical application of true love; the demonstration of peace; the acts that uphold the standard of justice; all these build up the consciousness of sanity in individuals, families, communities and nations. What about the opposite sides of these, namely, acrimony, division, hate, dichotomy, wickedness and injustice? These don't build up anyone in the journey of life; rather, they are catalysts to unpleasant situations in our world.

Instead of building up, these vicious elements, arising from the emotional systems of hate, destroy the fruits of individual and collective labour. He who builds on the platform of selfless Universal Love towards fellow earthmen, wherein lies God-Consciousness, works for his divine

ANNOTATION:
If you want mercy, show mercy to others.
Mercy begats mercy; hate begats wickedness.

ascent in the strata of existence and in the journey of life, both in the present earth- life and the realms beyond in the hereafter – the life beyond the physical aspects generally known.

Now, such a person – one embedded in the higher path of divine Love – is seen as enhancing the good of himself in specific divine terms. He is equally seen by the Forces of Light above as enhancing the good of all humans in general terms, as far as the divine spheres of reality is concerned. It is a plus factor with good rewards as one unfolds in the strata of existence. Enhancement of the good of our world is premised upon the practice of true Love, Peace and Justice.

THREE MODES OF MATERIAL NATURE

Dear earthmen, anyone who is situated in the mode of goodness on Earth, who upholds Love, Peace and Justice for all, is a major contributor to the 'Universal Pool of Probabilities', towards

ANNOTATION:
Blessed is the man seen by the Holy Spirit as working to enhance the good of all humans.
He will surely rise in the scale of the Almighty.

the rise of the earthmen in the Light of Heavenly realms. This is both in specific and general terms. Before we come back to the subject of the aforementioned pool of probabilities, let us take a brief look at the three modes of the material nature of being.

It is important to know that the earthmen on the physical realms of Earth are controlled by three modes of being. These include (i) the mode of ignorance – darkness – (ii) the mode of passion and (iii) the mode of goodness. This is the assertion of the sacred writings we know as Srimad-Bhagavatam and Upanishads, based on the spiritual declaration of the ancient Sanskrit 'acrayas', who received information from Extraterrestrial Intelligences of Light.

In the mode of ignorance (darkness), the earthman goes down both in the scale of being and in the journey of life. This is disadvantageous. However, the three modes of

ANNOTATION:
The sea of life is the pool of probabilities; therein dwells the earthman.
This is evident in each moment of existence.

nature– ignorance, passion and goodness – are the governing subtle principles that encapsulate all the factors and fabrics of existence in the world of man.

As far as existence is concerned, especially for the physical realms of Earth, you must be situated in one of these modes. Fluctuations may occur, however. In this case, the bad man of today becomes the good man of tomorrow, whilst the good man may revert into the system of the bad man, and so forth, in certain terms of mind volition.

Primarily, however, the major pre-dominating propensity of the mode of ignorance, is that the earthmen who are therein situated uphold the network of darkness, to the extent that their happiness are within the framework of the pain of others. In other words, they are happy to see other humans – especially their perceived enemies – in pain.

ANNOTATION:
***Darkness, passion or goodness rule the consciousness of man on the
physical realms of Earth. You are situated in one of these.***

When you cause pain to others, whether through prayers, violence, nepotism, amongst others, and become gratified in that consciousness, you are certainly in the mode of darkness. You must rise above this, in your own interest in the journey of life.

The psychology of this nature of being – the mode of ignorance – is the prime element that emboldens the network of the forces of darkness in the psychic spheres. It gives such vicious astral entities the metaphysical 'right' to use man against man. To this end, the mode of ignorance holds forth the core gestalt of all forms of killings, terrorism, wickedness and violence in the world of man.

The second aspect of the mode of nature, namely, the mode of passion, is the realm of temporal material aggrandisement and enjoyment. It is like a sea of mundane gratification governing the consciousness of multitudes of the earthmen.

ANNOTATION:
All forms of wickedness and vicious mental pattern arise from the repugnant mode of darkness. This mode leads downward in the journey of life.

The Great Lord Jesus the Christ referred to this mode as the embodiment of the mundane minds solely embedded and concentrated in seeking for **'what to eat, what to drink and what to put on'.** (See Math. 6:25 – 34).

It is easier for the earthman within the mode of passion to fall into the mode of darkness. In the mode of passion, selfishness is the order of the day; attachments to material things of the Earth-world isn't left out, amongst others. Whereas those in the mode of darkness go down in the journey of life, those situated within the mode of passion are held earth-bound in the universal scale of existence. The subject matter of 'earth-bound' is a topic for another day.

Suffice it to say that whether one goes down in the journey of life, or is held earth-bound, all constitutes varying degrees of delay to the ascent of any Soul in the human embodiment. And this delay holds forth degradation, predicaments

ANNOTATION:
Your food, clothes, houses, cars, positions, amongst others, are not the basis of existence, and do not accompany you into the realms beyond after physical death.

and unpleasant situations, even in the hereafter.

The mode of goodness is the upper aspects of the three modes of nature. When one is situated in the mode of goodness, he walks on the selfless path and sees to the good and wellbeing of others. And as good attracts good, good follows him in the journey of life. Religion is expected to play a major part in this aspect of being, but whether or not it does so, is not for me to judge. Who made me a judge?

Nevertheless, religion must be firm in leading humans on the path of goodness. It must lead on the true path of Love, Peace and Justice in mercy for all. It must avoid egotism as well as undue consciousness of superiority, while performing the task of leading humans along the path of goodness. It must be weary of the interference of the modes of both darkness and passion, set to keep religion in shambles.

ANNOTATION:
Organised religion should be a resting place for the minds of the earthman, but it has instead become a prison yard for the children of men.

However, religion alone is not the only framework for existence in the mode of goodness, though it has a vital role to play there. And the mode of goodness itself is not the ultimate mode available to Souls in the human embodiment. Within the three modes of nature – darkness, passion and goodness – the mode of goodness is the best and the highest. But beyond the three modes of material nature lies another mode, namely, the mode of divine nature.

The mode of goodness in the material world is different from the mode of divine nature, which operates beyond the material aspects of goodness. On one hand, it is easier for one to come from the mode of goodness to the transcendental platform of the mode of divine nature. On the other hand, if one is not careful while situated in the mode of goodness, his goodness will mingle with the mode of passion.

ANNOTATION:
Be a good man in your religion, and help your religion to imbibe and manifest the divine Light of the Almighty.

When your goodness is mingled with the mode of passion, it represents a certain kind of fall. Some people say: 'When I do good to others, they don't appreciate me'. That is not the kind of mind-set properly situated in the mode of goodness. For instance, when the act of goodness is shown solely for the purpose of human praise or appreciation, it is brought down to the mode of passion. Against this, Christ warned thus:

> *"Be careful not to practice your righteousness in front of others to be seen by them.*
>
> *"If you do, you will have no reward from your Father in heaven. So when you give to the needy, do not announce it with trumpets ... to be honored by others.*

ANNOTATION:
Seek not the praise of men in all that you do, for that will credit nothing into your spiritual account, which is more valid than the physical life you have.

"Truly I tell you, they have received their reward in full. But when you give to the needy, do not let your left hand know what your right hand is doing, so that your giving may be in secret. Then your Father, who sees what is done in secret, will reward you" (Math. 6:1—4; NIV).

In the mode of goodness, one upholds the consciousness of selfless service in love to others. But in the higher mode of divine nature, situated beyond the three-dimensional modes of material nature, one is not only situated in selfless service in love to others but, more than that, he is firmly situated in, and committed to, carrying out the divine orders of the Eternal Lord of the Universes of God. To this end, his entire awareness will be fixed solely in God-consciousness.

One in the mode of goodness sojourns within the benevolent

One in the mode of goodness sojourns within the benevolent cycle, as far as the journey of life is concerned. However, he is still embedded in certain kinds of limitations of Matter, Energy, Space and Time (MEST). He will rise beyond such limitations when persistence in the mode of goodness brings him up to the mode of divine nature.

Ultimate ascent in the journey of life, the unfoldment thereof of the Soul personality, is attained by the earthman when he comes to the mode of divine nature. This mode is completely divine and situated beyond the limitations of Matter, Energy, Space and Time (MEST). Religion still has a role to play here. In this connection, the core spiritual essence of the teachings of the Great Lord Jesus the Christ, bereft of the boundary of the human intellect and organised congregations, is of utmost significance. And in certain ancient oriental religious parlance, it is referred to as 'back to Godhead'. The 'born-again' true experience in some deeper aspects is equally situated in the mode of divine nature.

ANNOTATION:
The mode of divine nature, the domain of the Lord and His bona-fide representatives, is the true destination of Souls, which can be reached now in the world of man.

UNIVERSAL POOL OF PROBABILITIES

Now, dear reader, I earlier mentioned the **'universal pool of probabilities'**. This constitutes great divine chambers in the Heavenly realms of Light of the higher Planetary Systems. In these chambers are stored, in a state of divine potential, the energies of the thoughts, words and actions of divine Love enacted by humans on the physical realms of Earth. The actions embedded in Peace and Justice with mercy, are equally stored there. This is part of the hidden mysteries of existence.

These chambers, however, wherein the aforementioned energies are stored, have their individual and collective aspects. The individual aspect is related to what can rightly be called the 'spiritual account' of a person, while the collective aspect deals with the 'spiritual account' of a family, community, diverse nations and the Earth-world at large, amongst others.

ANNOTATION:
There are mysteries of life; what we don't know is more than what we know.
Thus, we should be prepared to know more.

The modus-operandi of the universal pool of probabilities works strictly under the Universal Law of the Probable Systems. The intricate workings of this Universal Law are not generally known to the earthmen in both human religions and sciences. Its workings, however, entails amongst other things that any divine intervention from above the Earth-world, coming individually to a person, or collectively to a group of persons, will first be situated in the realms of probabilities.

I am speaking in this connection about the intervention of Extraterrestrial Intelligences (Angelic Beings) of the Heavenly realms of Light. Certain intervention of God Himself, including His multitudinous divine manifestations in diverse realms of existence, is not ruled out in this regard. For instance, the Almighty LORD Jehovah gave a clue of this via Prophet Jeremiah in the Holy Scriptures thus:

ANNOTATION:
It is said that if you close your eyes while poor people are crying,
you won't see when rich people are laughing.

"If at any time I declare concerning a nation or a kingdom, that I will pluck up or break down and destroy it, and if that nation, concerning which I have spoken, turns from its evil, I will relent of the disaster that I intended to do to it. And if at any time I declare concerning a nation or a kingdom that I will build and plant it, and if it does evil in my sight, not listening to my voice, then I will relent of the good that I had intended to do to it" *(Jer. 18:7—10; ESV).*

The above Words of the Almighty LORD holds forth the primary divine basis of probabilities. This applies both to individual and collective terms. Here, as spoken by God through Jeremiah, the collective aspect as related to nations and kingdoms, which certainly includes communities, families, regions, and groups

ANNOTATION:
It is said: Do not blame the cobweb in the house, blame the spider that made it.
Do not blame another for what you have brought upon yourself.

of people, are involved. Nevertheless, in divine terms, this is also applicable to individuals.

Simply stated: the projected manifestation of any intended divine intervention stands first upon the threshold of probabilities. This means that the intervention, even when spoken of, may or may not occur, based on certain factors. The thoughts, words and actions of an intended beneficiary of the intervention, determine whether or not the promised or revealed intervention will be physically manifested. We must take note of this individually and collectively, because whether we like it or not, whether we know it or not, the immutable Universal Law of the Probable Systems must play out.

The Universal Law of the Probable Systems works by diverse factors. The factor determining the kind and degree of divine intervention that would be offered, is there. The factor of volition is there, determining the choice of thought,

ANNOTATION:
Earthman, don't look only for where you fell down, but look also for where you slipped before your fall.

from the pool of thoughts probabilities in the consciousness, that would be physically enacted, whether it is in tandem with the expected intervention.

Again, the factor of emotional energy behind every thought is there. If the electromagnetic energy of a thought not physically enacted is of greater intensity at any given moment than that of the thought physically realised, the energy of the unrealised thought constitutes another factor in the aforementioned pool of probabilities, amongst other factors.

As far as existence is concerned, in the light of eternal truth, there is nothing like accident; nothing like luck; nothing like chance. Because, as expressed by Saint Paul in the Bible: **"Be not deceived; God is not mocked: for whatsoever a man soweth, that shall he also reap"** (Gal. 6:7; KJV). This is based on the immutable Universal Law of Reciprocal Action, also known as the law of karma, or sowing and reaping, which we earlier discussed.

ANNOTATION:
He who sets his father's house on fire will have only ruins to inherit. He who troubles his house will inherit the wind.

This Universal Law of Reciprocal Action is implemented in all the Universes of God by the manifestations of the Almighty God dwelling in the higher Heavenly realms of Light. These manifestations of God are known as the 'Supreme Lords of Justice and Retribution'. These 'Supreme Lords' are so precise and capable of intercepting and registering the slightest thought of any creature, including the children of men, in any realm of the entire Universal Systems.

The 'Supreme Lords of Justice and Retribution', as earlier stated, are the manifestations of the Almighty God in the realms of the manifested Universes of God, especially amongst the dimension of the higher Extraterrestrial Intelligences. They are also known as 'The Universal Watchers' in certain divine terms.

It may be recalled that the great Extraterrestrial Intelligence, who spoke in the vision of King

Nebuchadnezzar, which he communicated to Prophet Daniel as recorded in the Holy Bible, was referred to as a 'Watcher'. This Watcher spoke about the decision of the hierarchy of Watchers and gave directives related to the projected predicaments of King Nebuchadnezzar in those days.

It should be noted, however, that such directives are carried out, as always the case, by other divine personalities in the Heavenly realms below the divine placement of the Watchers themselves. Thus, Prophet Daniel wrote:

> **"I saw in *the visions of my head upon my bed, and, behold, a Watcher and a holy one came down from Heaven. He cried aloud, and said thus, Hew down the tree, and cut off his branches, shake off his leaves, and scatter his fruits: let***

ANNOTATION:
Your stand at any moment in time determines the kind of focus on you from above.

the beasts get away from under it, and the fowls from his branches .... This matter is by the decree of the Watchers, and the demand by the word of the holy ones: to the intent that the living may know that the Most High ruleth in the kingdom of men...." (See Dan. 4:1—37).

Furthermore, the 'Supreme Lords of Justice and Retribution', who themselves are an aspect of direct manifestations of the One Eternal God, are in total control of all the chambers of the pool of probabilities in all the Universes of God. Whether such chambers are in the Heavenly realms of Light or in the den of the vicious astral forces, they cannot escape the aforementioned control of the Supreme Lords of Justice and Retribution.

ANNOTATION:
God is the Controller of all manifestations. He is all that is and the Source of all that is. He has diverse manifestations of Himself.

Now, in the order of Extraterrestrial existence of the Supreme Lords of Justice and Retribution, are also the 'Controllers of Initial Life Manifestations'. The 'Controllers of Initial Life Manifestations' are the 'Supreme Lords of Creation'. They are also the direct manifestations of the One Eternal God in that kind of reality and existence.

The Supreme Lords of Creation are the Holy Ones who created all things; they are the Ones who planted man on the physical realms of Earth. Remember the divine expression in the Holy Scripture related to the creation of man: **"And God said, Let us make man in our own image, after our likeness"** (Gen. 1:26). The word 'us' herein used, is very important in this connection.

The Supreme Lords of Creation, the Supreme Lords of Justice and Retribution, amongst other divine direct manifestations of God in the higher Heavenly realms of Light, operate in the divine gestalt of One Eternal Supreme Consciousness of God. It

ANNOTATION:
The One Eternal God has multidimensional aspects of Himself in the eternal validity of the Oneness of Himself.

must be known that, in the gestalt of this Supreme Consciousness, God is forever and ever One. In the Divine Oneness of God in all the multidimensional direct manifestations of the Sole Ultimate Reality – the One Eternal Source – God is One in Himself as All.

However, in the divine spheres, all the aforementioned 'Supreme Lords' work under the authority of 'One in the Centre'. Here, I am referring to the 'Eternal One' spoken of in the Holy Scriptures as **'King of Kings and Lord of Lords'**. He was set apart of old, in manifestation within the systems of gross matter, as the only One who will bring forth all the necessary divine conditions under which the earthmen and the Earth- world will flourish in the Light of Heavenly systems. This is part of the message given in this age to the earthmen via the one that writes this – **Harbinger of the Last Covenant.**

THE LORD'S UNIVERSAL HIERARCHY

The Supreme Lords of Creation, the Supreme Lords of Justice and Retribution, the Galactic Lords, the Solar Lords, amongst others, do reach out to the Earth-world in certain ways and terms, in the Name of God. They send to us some intermediary Heavenly Beings, to intervene for good in the affairs of the earthmen, whether to a person or group of people.

Some of these intermediaries are equally great Extraterrestrial Intelligences, such as the Angels, Archangels, Cherubims, amongst others. Again, some of these intermediaries, the Angelic Ones above, are born on Earth as humans in different parts of the world. Furthermore, **'The King of Kings and Lord of Lords'** Himself also does same, in certain terms of divine protocol. Apart from coming down from Heaven Himself, He sends intermediaries. Even the One above the 'Centre', who is above all, known as **'The Ancient of Days'** in the Holy Scriptures, does same.

ANNOTATION:
The network of cosmic divine administration is beyond the
comprehension of the earthman.

Most often, any communication between the 'Supreme Lords' and the Earth-world must be done via other Extraterrestrial intermediaries. In this case, an earthman must be involved, as far as the message, intervention or objective is designed for the Earth-world and the earthmen. Thus, an earthman will be linked to an Extraterrestrial intermediary, who in turn will be linked to the dimension of the Supreme Lords. The earthmen involved here must be divinely chosen and prepared. These are some of the hidden mysteries playing out in our world, unknown to the multitude in diverse religions and scientific enclaves.

Some aspects of the Holy Scriptures and sacred writings were given to the earthmen in this manner, throughout the ages, in different parts of our world. However, the misrepresentation of the earthmen, arising from misinterpretation of some of these information, have in some instances led to the quest for religious dominance

ANNOTATION:
The Scriptures are given from above to guide man on the path of Light. Reading the Scripture in itself, with the intention of spiritual development in Light, is action in the mode of goodness.

cum misguided psychological propensity for mental religious supremacy, intense greed, war, killings, amongst others, in the guise of upholding religious tenets, tradition and belief systems.

Nevertheless, regardless of man's irresponsible behaviour on the physical realms of Earth, the Lord of the Universe and the Great Ones in the Heavenly realms of Light above have not and will not abandon us. Thus, in one of such conversations in our time, a Supreme Lord spoke via intermediary Extraterrestrial Intelligence to a certain human on Earth, which gives a clue of the nature, reality and existence of the Supreme Lords themselves. He said thus:

> ***"We are the voices who speak without tongues of our own. We are Sources of that Energy from which you came.***

ANNOTATION:
A glimpse into the nature and consciousness of higher realities above the world of man.

"We are Creators, yet we have also been created. We seeded your Universe as you seed other realities.

"We do not exist in your historical terms, nor have we known physical existence.

"Our joy created the exaltation from which your world comes. Our existence is such that communication must be made by others to you.

"Verbal symbols have no meaning for us. Our experience is not translatable. We hope our intent is. In the vast infinite scope of consciousness, all is possible.

ANNOTATION:
"Our experience is not translatable". That is the nature of higher Universal realities. And as above, so below.

"There is meaning in each thought. We perceive your thoughts (thoughts of Divine Love) as lights. They form patterns.

"Because of the difficulties of comm unication, it is nearly impossible for us to explain our reality.

"Know only that we exist. We send immeasurable vitality to you, and support all of these structures of consciousness with which you are familiar.

"You are never alone. We have always sent emissaries to you who understand your needs. Though you do not know us, we cherish you". (Note: Source withheld).

ANNOTATION:
"There is meaning in each thought". This is part of the last lessons that we must learn and master in the world of man, before further progress into higher dimensions.

FACTOR OF PROBABILITIES

Sometimes the earthman thinks thus: 'If there is God or Lord of the Universe, as well as Holy Angels guiding our lives and our world, why don't they take away all our problems?' Some people think that terrorism, kidnapping, corruption, man's inhumanity to man and all forms of violence and wickedness should just be taken away by God or His holy Angels, without our involvement.

We, the children of men, must know that things don't happen that way in all the Universes of God. If that is the way things occur, then all the unpleasant situations in the Earth-world would have vanished for long, without the people of our generation coming to the physical realm to notice such. Now, on one hand, we are in a

ANNOTATION:
In the higher divine terms, answers can be given to man's mundane questions that are in themselves completely meaningless.

'school' on Earth and we must learn. On the other hand, we will certainly get to the required universal destination, whether or not we fail now in the school of life, for as long as any given failure teaches us how not to fail again.

We, the children of men, must work hard, in divine terms, to bring forth the basis of divine intervention that will salvage us – save us from ourselves. We must know that things like divine intervention are based on the right of divine intervention which Angelic Ones above obtain from the pool of probabilities, arising from human thoughts, words and actions.

When a person or group of persons in the mode of ignorance enact the thoughts, words or actions of wickedness, the vicious energies arising from these are also stored in the chambers of the forces of darkness in the astral realms. This is

ANNOTATION:
Failure is not good for man; the only good therein is that it should teach man how not to fail again.

where the right of astral attacks against the earthmen, individually and collectively, is obtained by the forces of darkness – the most vicious astral entities.

The probabilities involved here have to do with the degree of divine intervention to be provided in Light, for the benefit of humans; the degree of attack that may come against humans from the vicious astral entities, amongst others. Individually and collectively, we, the children of men, are the determining factors of our beneficial or malignant experiences in the world of man. Simply put: We are responsible for all that is happening in our world.

Overall, the earthman is placed in the position where he and he alone, through his thoughts, words and actions, is the originator of whatever happens to him. Man is responsible for whatsoever that happens to him, whether from the realms of Light or from the den of darkness; whether or not he knows this. That is why man

ANNOTATION:
We either form a sane world of love or destroy ourselves in the vicious cycle of hate. The choice is ours.

must be saved from himself, necessitating this letter to the earthmen – **save us from ourselves.**

Oscar Wilde, renowned Irish philosopher, said: **"I must say to myself that I ruined myself; for none can be ruined safe by his own hands".** That is true. To this end, the ancient Egyptian Hermit, Matheno, a wise man who, unknown to many, taught John the Baptist while he was a boy, in the cave of king David at Engedi, said about the earthman thus:

> *"He may attain the greatest heights, or sink to deepest depths; for what he wills to gain he has the power to gain.*

> *"If he desires strength he has the power to gain that strength; but he must encounter resistances to reach the goal; no strength is ever gained in idleness.*

ANNOTATION:
Be conscious of your thoughts. Thought is the only activity that is real; it gives rise to words and actions.

"So, in the whirl of many-sided conflicts man is placed where he must strive to extricate himself.

"In every conflict man gains strength; with every conquest he attains to greater heights.

"With every day he finds new duties and new cares.

"Man is not carried over dangerous pits, nor helped to overcome his foes. He is himself his army, and his sword and shield; and he is captain of his hosts" (Aquarian Gospel 14:11—15).

ANNOTATION:
Obstacles are stepping stones on the path of divine ascent.
Blessed is the man who understands this.

He who follows the destructive path of wickedness, will be encapsulated by destruction and experience same in the journey of life, whether or not he knows it, in this world or hereafter. This works strictly in accordance with the immutable Universal Laws of the **One Eternal Seed-Giving- Father** of all realities, all existences, the Almighty. Such a person is on the downward path in the scale of being; the experience is very dangerous for any Soul personality, namely, the mode of darkness.

We are admonished to do good at all times, so that good will follow us always, here and hereafter. For ages, so many children of men have followed the vicious path of hate, injustice and violence. This vicious path has stored in the probable systems great rights for the attacks of the forces of darkness in the world of man. These forces of darkness, great vicious entities of the astral realms, operate via multitude of the earthmen, who have their nature – mode of darkness – propensities and inclinations.

ANNOTATION:
You are either on the path of ascent or the downward path in the journey of life.

It can't be otherwise.

Terrorism, rape, kidnapping, arson, cultism, armed robbery, oppression, greed, war, hate, viruses, corruption, human trafficking, hard drug, tribalism, amongst other vicissitudes, are great impediments limiting the earthmen. These are caused by the earthmen, limiting humans, individually and collectively, from rising into the divine 'stardom' of our essential higher aspects.

These are amongst the unpleasant situations that we must be saved from. And as we seek divine intervention to emancipate us from these things – to save us from ourselves – we must understand that divine intervention only comes solely in proportion to the right we give for such intervention.

MECHANISMS OF DIVINE INTERVENTION

Now, divine intervention from above to us, the children of men, individually or collectively,

ANNOTATION:
It is said that when you cry for rain you are crying for mud as well. Those who refuse to forgive break the bridges on which they must pass.

is predicated upon what is done on Earth by us to bring about the intervention. Divine intervention certainly can't be otherwise. There are great Extraterrestrial Intelligences – mighty Angelic Beings of Light – the Spirits of God in the Heavenly realms, who are capable of giving helping hand in the affairs of this world.

These Intelligences of Divine Light above exist at different levels and hierarchy in the Power of the Almighty. They have great spiritual Power, but they are not permitted by divine laws to directly intervene and ameliorate all the predicaments of the earthmen. They have the Power of God to do this, but by divine laws they can't act arbitrary to end all the sufferings of men.

The mighty Forces of Light in the Heavenly realms only act in our affairs on Earth strictly within the ambit of specific things we have done on Earth that raise the standard and divine

ANNOTATION:
*Even the United Nations can't arbitrarily intervene and send a
peace keeping force to a nation without following certain processes.
Heaven does same for Earth and more in certain divine terms.*

legality for their intervention. Even God Himself act in this manner, for that is the rule of being. The intervention of the Forces of Light is based upon what is recorded for man, as far as his selfless actions, words and thoughts of Love for God and man are concerned.

This right of divine intervention on Earth is granted within the storage of Love, Peace and Justice in mercy, within the chambers of Light. Now, this right of divine intervention is obtained by the Forces of Light from the 'universal pool of probabilities', strictly under the Universal Law of the Probable Systems.

This Law itself is God in motion in all the Universes of God. And the pool of probabilities, which is a fundamental aspect of God, represents in certain terms the 'sea of life' in which humans dwell. As fish lives in water, so the lives of the earthmen are completely embedded with the 'universal waters' of probabilities.

ANNOTATION:
Selfless actions of love are urgently needed now than ever for the deliverance of the world of man.

Even then, the degree, kind or measure of divine intervention offered to the earthmen, individually and collectively, from above, in any issue in the world of man, varies. This depends on the measure of right obtained by Heaven, the right which we give to Heaven, the limit thereof, at any given point of divine intervention. And within the subtle intricacies of this measurement lies the aforementioned probabilities.

For example, if there is a projected terrorist attack on a certain area of our Planet, that would take the lives of a thousand people, and divine intervention comes in, certain things will happen based upon the approved measure of intervention from the pool of probabilities. Now, the divine intervention may banish the attack from occurring at all, in this case some earthmen wouldn't know what happened from above. They wouldn't know that there was a divine intervention in the first place.

ANNOTATION:
You can't run beyond your shadow; you can't give what you don't have.

There is also the possibility that, instead of the attack to take a thousand lives, based upon the measure of the right of divine intervention obtained, about three hundred people may die, while seven hundred people are salvaged. In this case some people wouldn't know that there was divine intervention at all, because of the deaths that occurred. Things like this happen in our world; they happen in our individual lives and the lives of our collective existence.

Let it be emphasized that our selfless divine service of Love to our fellow men and to every creature, gives the Forces of Light the divine right to intervene on Earth, in one way or another. Our thoughts, words and actions of Love towards the Creator and the created, are of utmost importance in this regard.

Whatever you do in Love to help others will never be passed over lightly by the mighty Forces of Light in the Heavenly realms. Our selfless prayers in Love for others, which are

ANNOTATION:
Without certain kind of divine intervention,
the Earth Planet would have been destroyed for long.

channels of giving out our spiritual energies for the good of others, contribute along this line in no small measure. That is why the Great Lord Jesus the Christ admonished the earthmen thus:

> ***"But I say unto you, Love your enemies, bless them that curse you, do good to them that hate you, and pray for them which despitefully use you, and persecute you"*** *(Math. 5:44; KJV).*

The above is one of the greatest messages from Heaven ever given to the children of men. The Lord came down from Heaven to guide us on the path of divine ascent. He admonished us on the rudiments wherein lies the plus factor of being; the path in which is inherent the fundamental basis for Heavenly divine intervention in the world of man.

ANNOTATION:
When the earthman is told to love his enemies, he lacks the divine wisdom required to comprehend the core essence of this ultimate admonition.

TAKE A STAND NOW

Therefore, with the little span of life left for each and every earthman, let us use same to walk on the sure foundation path that is designed to salvage us from ourselves. We have to do this knowing that whatever we must be saved from, are the things that we have set up against ourselves, knowingly or unknowingly.

We must make the choice either to build in Love, Peace and Justice or destroy ourselves in hate, wickedness and injustice. We must choose to build and not to destroy. As individuals, we must face the reality of this in our diverse families, enclaves, communities and nations, in the full knowledge that, it is much easier to destroy than to build. And the act of destruction, said to be easier to this end, hangs upon the perpetrator, the prime elements of destruction in the journey of life, here or hereafter.

ANNOTATION:
Why do we choose to use our little span of life on the physical
realms of Earth to destroy rather than to build?

Peace is absolutely imperative, if individuals and nations of the Earth-world must make the required divine progress, wherein lies the essence of existence. Love is absolutely necessary if any individual, family or nation must excel in the world of man, in the Light of the Almighty God. By Justice, the balance between the seen and unseen, upholding the nectar of being, creating a sense of goodness and oneness, is enacted.

An African adage has it that **"Peace is like a blanket: when you put it on you get warmth"** (for therein lies true progress and development of life); **"when you take it off you get cold"**; this is disastrous, in which the meaning of progress, development and collective wellbeing is defeated. What the world lacks is Love, Peace and Justice in mercy. The world is not in lack of mundane things – houses, cars, money, clothes, food, drinks, amongst others.

ANNOTATION:
The greatest truths are the simplest ones.
The hand that knows how to give will always gather.

LIMITED EFFORTS

Earthmen, this treatise is designed, amongst other things, to throw more light on the physical and the subtle aspects of Peace in general terms, but with specific emphasis on abating all forms of wickedness, as related to the subject matter of this message. We need lasting Peace, Justice and Love in the world of man. The governments of diverse nations are doing their utmost best to achieve these, but how far can they go in human terms? The evidence of how far they can go is there for all to see on Earth.

The efforts of government in this connection, embedded within the framework of human frailties as it is, are fraught with limitations and thus will not achieve the ultimate desired goal in divine terms. The aforementioned ultimate goal is absolute, not relative. No government in the world of man can give absolute Love, Peace and Justice to the children of men.

ANNOTATION:
Think more of what you will contribute to build our world and less of what our world will contribute to build you up.

Whereas we must appreciate the efforts of different governments of the Earth-world towards Peace and Justice, however, we need something far more than the efforts of governments of the nations to achieve absolute Peace. The people of this world now are in dire need of the Holy Spirit of the One Eternal Almighty God to give us absolute Peace, individually and collectively.

We must work to bring forth the Spirit of Love in action for Peace and Justice to reign on Earth. Let it be emphasized that without the Finger of the Holy Spirit, the expectation of achieving real Love, Peace and Justice in the world of man will be futile.

In this expectation, however, we have our individual and collective roles to play towards peaceful co-existence. Our roles will enable us, in accordance with the inexorable Universal Law of Homogeneity, to cooperate with the Holy Spirit. In the Holy Spirit alone lies the

ANNOTATION:
The Holy Spirit is the final solution to all the vicissitudes of the children of men.

Divine Potency to deliver us; to save us from ourselves.

On one hand, Love brings Peace; on the other hand, Justice encapsulates both Peace and Love, whilst hate brews wickedness. For instance, the elements of terrorism on the physical realms of Earth are core agents of hate in our world. We must rise up and lift these our human brothers and sisters in prayers for transformation. We must pray for the Holy Spirit, not to destroy them, but to transform them into the path of goodness in Light.

The nature of Love, Peace and Justice in mercy, brings Love, Peace and Justice in mercy to the children of men. The nature of wickedness brings wickedness. We must rise above the lower nature of the beasts embedded in violence. We must align ourselves with the nature of the Forces of Light above willing to help us. We must extricate ourselves from the nature of the forces

ANNOTATION:
Pray for the transformation of the vicious minded people; it is a major contribution to the path of Light.

of darkness above man working assiduously to subjugate us.

We must know that some factors of existence, in certain terms, are premised upon the intricate web of battles, especially in the material modes of passion and ignorance. The forces of darkness themselves are situated in these modes. Their nature, in conjunction with the multitude of humans in their platform, brings us down to the violent realms of the beasts.

In all these, certain aspects of existence are entangled in an intricate web of battles for survival. We will take a look at this in the next segment of this material, before we return to more valid points related to the subject matter of this treatise in subsequent segments.

God bless the reader.

ANNOTATION:
No one holds you down but yourself. Therefore, free yourself from the material mode of darkness.

A MAN'S GREATEST BATTLES ARE THE ONES HE FIGHTS WITHIN HIMSELF.

- The Harbinger

ANNOTATION:
One does not drown by falling into water but by staying too long therein.

UNIFYING DIVINE REALITY

Dear reader, this segment deals briefly on the intricate webs of battles in both the physical and the subtle aspects of the world, and to some extent the Universe at large. A point is expected to be

ANNOTATION:
The English proverb says: 'United we stand, but divided we fall'.
Earthman, it is said that when the threads unite they can tie the lion.

noted in this segment, but related to the overall theme of this letter, even as we proceed with the foregoing subject – **save us from ourselves** – in subsequent segments.

Now, on one hand, it is said that a woman may be focused on how to prepare a plantain and eat, but on the other hand, the plantain may be focused on how to cause her pain in the belly. This is part of the intricate webs of battles, as far as existence is concerned, namely, the battle of survival. Failure to apply Love, Peace and Justice in mercy to the means for survival on Earth, place the earthmen in the cycle of suffering.

Lord Gautama Buddha said: **"All conditioned things are impermanent --- when one sees this with wisdom, one turns away from suffering"** (Dhammapada verse 277). The wisdom mentioned here is the consciousness encapsulating Love, Peace and Justice in mercy. Without these, the earthmen won't end the vicious cycle of suffering inherent in the mundane quest for survival.

Thus, the Great Lord Jesus the Christ once admonished: **"Blessed are the merciful: for they shall obtain mercy"** (Math. 5:7; KJV). This is the foremost basis of excellence in the Light of the Almighty God, for obtaining mercy in the journey of life. In this lies the unifying divine reality for all existences. In the family, community, and in all that you do to your fellow earthmen, as well as with the lesser creatures of God, endeavour to show mercy for your own good.

The earthmen on the Islamic path also have this beautiful quote on mercy thus: **"Those who are merciful will be shown mercy by the Most Merciful. Be merciful to those on the earth and the One in the heavens will have mercy upon you"** (Sunan al-Tirmidhi). Mercy encapsulates all that dwells on the benevolent mode of goodness.

ANNOTATION:
"Blessed are the merciful: for they shall obtain mercy". Let no one pass over this lightly in the journey of life.

Whosoever wants mercy to be shown to him, let him first of all show mercy to others. Love, Peace and Justice are embedded in mercy. You want to be loved, but you have no love for your fellow earthmen; you do not love even the little creatures of the Almighty; it doesn't work that way. In all that we do, the Universal Law of Reciprocal Action must play out, no matter how long.

You can't give peace to others when you do not have peace within your heart. Those in the mode of darkness can't ever possess peace within, talk less of giving it to others. How can you have peace when through your thoughts, words and actions the hearts of some earthmen are in constant pain. You torment others with your actions, even with your words and prayers; you torment what you think you are higher than, what about what is higher than you?

ANNOTATION:
In all that you do, and whoever you are, always remember that there are powers ahead of you in the scale of the Almighty.

BE READY TO LEARN AND GROW

I am beginning to learn to be more careful in life and to refrain from tormenting not only my fellow men but also the lesser creatures of the Almighty. I know that many have mastered this and are far ahead of me in this regard, but I am nonetheless willing to learn and grow. For instance, one day I saw a cockroach around where I was seated. It was just one cockroach moving around and attempting to climb up to my shoe. As I took something to kill it, I clearly heard the voice of the Lord, and He said to me:

"Harbinger of the Last Covenant, spare the life of the cockroach in My mercy. Behold, as you are higher in the scale of life than the life-stream you know as cockroach, so several life- streams are higher than your human form in My scale of being. Show mercy on what is lesser than

ANNOTATION:
In whatever state or dimension that you are situated in existence --
Angel, Spirit or Human -- you are in a state of becoming.
Thus, there are always things ahead to know about.

you, and you will obtain mercy from what is higher than you".

Then I let the cockroach go and prayed for forgiveness and mercy of the Lord. This is an aspect of divine knowledge that some of us are ignorant of. But fire will certainly burn the hand of a child who touches it, whether or not the child knows what it is. The fire won't say 'oh, this is an ignorant child, let me not burn the hand'. Things do not work that way in existence.

At that point also, following my experience with the cockroach, I remembered an important lesson which the masters of the ancient Vedic sacred writings taught the earthmen. This has to do with the experience of a certain wise man. The wise man, said to be a 'holy one', was reportedly situated on the path of Light, in accordance with the level of Light shown to his part of the world at that time.

ANNOTATION:
In the Holy Bible, God said:
"My people are destroyed for lack of knowledge" (Hos. 4:6).
Spiritual ignorance is the prime propensity of the mode of
darkness.

It is important to note that part of the earthly mission of the Great Lord Jesus the Christ – **the Light of the world** – was to usher in greater aspects of the Light of the Almighty God into the world of man. This is for the guidance of all generations of the children of men. But before His coming, there were some degrees of Light brought to the Earth-world by the Spirit of God via some earthmen in diverse places, whether or not this is known in organised religious terms.

Even after the coming of the Great Lord Jesus the Christ, there were subsequent manifestations of God's divine Light via some earthmen at diverse degrees. The Lord Himself gave a clue to this thus: **"Wherefore, behold, I send unto you prophets, and wise men, and scribes"** (Math. 23:34; KJV). The ones mentioned by the Lord in this connection, are embedded in the Light of God at diverse levels.

ANNOTATION:
Christ, in all ramifications of His core identity, in all His multitudinous manifestations, in all generations, is the divine Light of this world.

Now, the wise man mentioned in the Vedic sacred writings was a confidential adviser to the King of that jurisdiction. Thus, he was very close to the King. In that community, however, there was a notorious robber who assaulted and robbed the daughter of the king. The notorious thief was declared wanted dead or alive. However, the robber ran to the wise man and confessed his evil deeds, whilst declaring his willingness to change for good.

For a while, the wise man kept the bad man in his house, solely admonishing him on the need to completely refrain from criminality. The wise man intended to present the robber thereafter to the king and plead for mercy on his behalf. But before this was done, the king got a report that the wanted rogue was in the house of the wise man. Consequently, he ordered their arrests and at last they were brought before him.

In anger the king further ordered their execution, but with specific emphasis on how

ANNOTATION:
Earthman, when the leading frog falls into a pit, others behind take caution.

the wise man should be killed. He directed that a strong long stick should be forced into the anus of the wise man and brought out through his mouth. The king felt betrayed by the wise man, for harbouring the wanted criminal. He never gave the wise man the opportunity to explain the true situation of what transpired.

The wise man was terrified to hear about the kind of death experience that awaited him. The night before the execution, he prayed and cried to the Almighty God, desiring to know what he did that attracted that kind of death. The wise man knew, however, that nothing happens by chance and that we reap what we sow.

In the course of his prayers, an Angelic Being from above manifested and gave him a divine revelation which, amongst other things, clarified the basis of that nature of death assigned to him. What happened was that when the wise man

ANNOTATION:
The man who does not stand near the snake is the one who says:
'shake it'. One who seeks revenge digs two graves.

was a boy, he was in the habit of killing grasshoppers. He would catch grasshoppers, pass a stick through their anus to the mouth and line them up in that manner, causing them painful death.

In his terms as a boy, it was a mere play, but this 'play' brought about the painful death of many grasshoppers in his hands. At a certain stage, it was signed and sealed by the Supreme Lords of Justice and Retribution that his own death on the physical realms of Earth would come in like manner.

The Angelic Being made it known to him that the painful death, which awaited him, will not hinder him from having benevolent life after death experience. He was told that his abode in the Paradise after death is guaranteed, because of his enormous good works.

However, it was clearly made known to him that the coming manner of his death won't be

ANNOTATION:
Extraterrestrial Intelligences of Light have always guided the earthman on the path of divine knowledge.

changed, unless it is set aside by a higher divine intervention from God above the divine authority and hierarchy of the Supreme Lords of Justice and Retribution, which rarely comes. At last the wise man died in the manner that was said.

CAMOUFLAGE SYSTEMS OF REALITY

Listen, dear earthman: you cannot be taller than a person and be shorter than him at the same time. If you are taller than a man, know that he is shorter than you. What he is at that point is what you are not; and what you are, is what he is not. I am saying this in the light of the camouflage systems of existence, from the least to the greatest creatures in all the Universes of God.

Beyond all facets of the camouflage systems, including the world of man, lies the divine principles unifying all creatures, all realities, all manifestations, in the One Eternal Spirit that we

ANNOTATION:
The camouflage systems of reality harbour the limited aspects of being. Your core identity transcends the camouflage realities.

call 'God'. Consequently, on one hand God is 'All That Is', on the other hand, God, in the eternal essence of His Prime Identity, is forever beyond all that is.

Apart from the divine principles unifying all things, by which all things are within all things, in which God is all in all, even within the apparent camouflage systems, the factors underlining the unifying basis of existence are evident. Those living on the platform of goodness, upholding Peace, Love and Justice in mercy to all, are situated on the platform of the consciousness beyond the camouflage systems.

In the first place, you must know that there are more than the eyes can see. What the eyes can see is the camouflage of what the eyes can't see. In certain terms, the Earth Planet – the world of man – the realm wherein we are, is a field of battle, in both her physical and subtle aspects. Extraterrestrial Intelligences have made it known that in our Solar System, the Earth-World is the

---

ANNOTATION:
*All things in all the Universes are united in the One Eternal Source
we call 'God'. The apparent divisions are within manifestations.*

war zone of mighty spirit beings.

The wars of the Forces of Light and the forces of darkness, occurring beyond the camouflage systems, affect humans in diverse ways. This depends on where each person is situated, whether in mode of ignorance, passion or goodness. This determines what each person attracts to himself. And within the overall gestalt of these modes, we collectively attract certain events to our world, in diverse jurisdictions, within the ambit of mass production.

Now, when you hear that a particular country is fighting war, certain areas may be the specific war zone, thus, excluding other areas of the country. For instance, today my country Nigeria is at war against Boko Haram, but the war zone is some areas in the North East. When the United States fought war in Iraq, the war zone was in some areas of Iraq.

ANNOTATION:
As far as the Earth Planet is concerned, the war of the Forces of Light and the forces of darkness, the final aspects thereof, will be brought to completion in this era.

Therefore, as far as the Solar System is concerned, as far as this particular Universe is concerned, including even some areas of the Galactic System, the Earth Planet is the war zone. This is the assertion of great Extraterrestrial Intelligences of Light who know better. These Intelligences have their order of existence, experience and realities far beyond the material body camouflage of the children of men.

There are vicious and powerful Extraterrestrial Intelligences – forces of darkness – in battle against the children of men, especially in the zone of the astral realms of Earth. There are also some powerful Forces of Light in battle against them to help humans. All these battles, however, whether for or against humans, the outcome thereof, depends on what man does on the physical realms of Earth. This is by virtue of the Universal Laws. But even as I speak now, mighty wars are raging in the astral realms of Earth.

ANNOTATION:
The Bible say: "Woe to the inhabiters of the earth and of the sea!
for the devil is come down unto you" (Rev. 12:12).

Now, Extraterrestrial Intelligences of divine Light, at different degrees and levels, are spread in all the Planetary Systems. However, searching to see these Mighty Ones of Eternal Light by our mundane spacecraft will always be futile, as they reside on a shield of invisibility beyond human space probes. The denizens of the Heavenly realms of Light, whether they reside in Mars, Venus, Saturn, amongst other variegated unlimited realms of the cosmic manifestations, can't be assessed by human space probes. Even the vicious astral entities can't be seen in that manner.

THE REALM OF BATTLES

Earthmen, critical look at our world and the life-forms therein shows clearly the evidence of battles. For instance, the moment you are born on Earth, you enter into a field of battle, whether you know it or not. If you study the rudiments of your conception in the womb, you will observe the elements of battle. Your emergence on

ANNOTATION:
There are even some Extraterrestrial Intelligences of Light, under diverse assignments, residing in the hidden recesses of the subtle realms of Earth.

Earth, through your physical birth, is your first victory in the battle field of the physical realms of Earth.

Consider the sexual activity between your parents that brought about your conception in the womb. You may be aware that when such a thing is done, the semen released from your father into your mother carries millions of cells. Now, each of these cells struggles in a related kind of battle to emerge as an identity – a personality in the physical world that we know.

Thus, your birth is a victory won in a battle fought in the realm of cells. The other cells that didn't emerge in the course of your conception, were defeated in the aforementioned battle. All the cells, each fought in certain terms to become human, but you defeated them all by Providence. So you can see the primordial origin of the battles of the earth-life.

ANNOTATION:
A chance is given to you, through your physical birth, to unfold in the spiritual essence of the school of life; don't misuse it.

The battles of the earth-life, especially as related to us the earthmen, started there in the realm of cells; it goes beyond there and continues after there. As an earthman, you will continue to fight for more victories in the journey of life. You will continue to fight more battles, yes, but as you grow in the dimension of your higher essential aspect, you will realize that the battles now and ahead are not that of guns and bombs. Rather, you will understand that upholding Love, Peace and Justice in mercy gives you victory in the battle for ascent in the journey of life.

Earthman, in this world, there are authorities at different levels and fields of human endeavour, which may be consulted for different purposes. Like when your health is challenged, you may consult a doctor; if you have an issue that deals with the legal system, you may consult a lawyer. You won't consult your doctor to attend to you in an issue regarding the legal system, neither

ANNOTATION:
Seek not the victory of life where it is not. Rather, seek it in love, peace, justice and mercy for all.

will you consult your pastor to pilot your flight from Nigeria to the United States.

When you talk about your essential aspects of being, which is spiritual, namely, your Higher Self, which has to do with your true multidimensional identity, who would you consult? You must know that the qualities of Peace, Love, Justice and Mercy flows from your Higher Self. But to comprehend the imperatives of these, who would you consult for guidance? Don't pass over this lightly. Remember, if you consult your doctor when sick and some medicines are prescribed for you, you have to take them with some measure of confidence, because your doctor is an authority in his field.

When we talk about the Universe or Universes, the true nature of existence and your core identity, who do we consult for authentic clarification? What about the true nature of the core of Planet Earth and her subtle aspects, as well as the subtle realities of the Planetary Systems?

ANNOTATION:
It is the Lord and His bona-fide representatives that guide man into the path of higher divine knowledge.

Who will guide the earthmen to understand the inner psychological propensity, reality and framework of multifarious humanoids in other systems beyond the physical realms? How would the earthman comprehend the nature of forces, whether of Light or darkness, beyond the physical world, including but not limited to their battles for the 'soul of Earth', amongst other things? What about where we are coming from and where we are going to?

To understand these amongst other mysteries of being, we must consult bona-fide spiritual authorities. In this case, there are masterminds – Saints, Sages, Prophets – who have given some clues to guide us in this connection. Also, there are Extraterrestrial Intelligences (Angelic Beings of God's Light) above our world who are willing to help us to know and act better.

ANNOTATION:
If you don't know where you are coming from, how would you know your destination?

Above all, there are manifestations of God at diverse stages in different realms. They establish the fundamental principles for the existence of the earthmen in the true order of divine Light. They guide as many as wishes to seek for guidance on divine ascent in the journey of life. They provide guidance not only for existence in the mode of goodness, but also for the establishment of the children of men in the eternal mode of divine nature. The case of the Great Lord Jesus the Christ is of utmost importance in this connection.

Now, the sayings and guidance provided for us by all the aforementioned, for the purpose of achieving victory in the battles of life, and for ascent in the journey of life, are there. They are well documented in the Holy Scriptures and in diverse sacred writings. We have to constantly assess the Holy Scriptures and the sacred writings for proper guidance on the need to live in love and peace on Earth.

ANNOTATION:
Peaceful co-existence of all humans, is the reality we must first uphold before having access to greater Universal realities in the higher Planetary Systems.

All the aforementioned also are fully aware, in the light of eternal truth, that there is no superior spiritual authority to guide man beyond his multidimensional core identity, namely, the Spirit which is man, which is God in man, and which is eternally one with God. Thus, man is often told to listen to his Spirit – his essential higher divine nature – in all that he does.

However, how many earthmen are properly situated to assess that innermost core aspects of themselves? In the midst of multitudinous simultaneous agitations arising from the mind faculties, the intellect, the emotional aspects, amongst others, the earthman often finds it difficult to listen to his Spirit. Thus, both oral and written guidelines must be provided for him at this present stage, representing in symbolic and literal terms of our world the 'mother' of divine knowledge for his guidance.

Now, if you don't know your father, who is the final authority that you should ask? You don't have to go to the chief of your village to ask

ANNOTATION:
There is no authority in the Universe, to guide you, beyond your higher essential divine aspect, which is your core identity.

whom your father is. The bona-fide authority to ask in this connection is your mother. And as far as spiritual knowledge is concerned, as far as man doesn't know himself, the Holy Scriptures and the sacred writings constitute the mother of his divine knowledge. And what did the Scripture say concerning the Earth as a field of battle? It says:

"For we are not fighting against human beings but against the wicked spiritual forces in the heavenly world, the rulers, authorities, and cosmic powers of this dark age" (Eph. 6:12; GNB).

Earthman, when you hear things like this, as spoken by Saint Paul in the Bible, don't pass over it lightly. Don't say to yourself, 'this doesn't matter', because it matters a great deal. Every earthman is in a battle field, but it is not a battle of flesh and blood. When you raise the standard of battle, in the use of guns, bombs, and other

ANNOTATION:
There are mighty forces of darkness in serious battle against the world of man.

material instruments against fellow earthmen, you are on the downward path in the journey of life.

In such instances, unknown to you, however, you are fighting towards your ultimate defeat, whether or not you gain human victory in such mundane battles. The instruments for victory in the battles of life going on in the world of man, are Love, Peace and Justice in mercy. Imbibe these divine qualities and you will receive the needed help from above, to be extricated from the intricate webs of battles, otherwise you will fail.

RELATIVE AND ABSOLUTE ASPECTS

Now, dear reader, the intricate webs of battles, within and beyond the world of man, have their relative and absolute aspects. Firstly, the relative aspect of battle has to do with the experience that some people have, in the cycle of sowing and reaping what we sow, but interpreted in human terms along the line of spiritual battles. Secondly, the absolute aspect has to do mostly

ANNOTATION:
It is said that the Master appears when the disciple is ready.
Don't stand against what has risen to help you.

with the quest for survival, which constitutes a battle of some kind.

However, some of the experiences of life, causing pain or death to some creatures, including humans, in the light of the battles of life, are unintentional to some extent. Some personalities who enact the battles in this terms do not see what they do in the light of any battle, yet it occurs. In existence, the normal activity of some higher beings, enacted for their survival and not intended in any way to cause harm or death, can still cause harm or death.

In this terms, therefore, the creatures higher than humans can unintentionally cause pain or death to humans. Though, in this case, the Universal Laws must subsist. And humans can also unintentionally cause pain or death to the lesser creatures; all occurring, however, within the ambit of the intricate webs of the battles of existence.

ANNOTATION:
Nothing escapes the Universal Laws in all the Universes of God; the Universal Laws are God in motion.

For example, if you are cooking, you may wash something with hot water and pour the hot water outside. This hot water may be poured unintentionally on some creatures such as ants and they die. Now, from the point of view of such ants, what you have done is a battle from 'above' against their realms. Some battles in existence are structured in this manner. When you look at existence from this reference point, you will observe that at diverse stages of consciousness battles occur.

For further example, a hungry lion may intentionally pursue an antelope to kill. On one hand, the lion thinks: 'Oh God I am hungry; thank You for giving me this antelope as food'. On the other hand, the antelope prays: 'Oh God save me from this lion'. From the antelope's point of view, the lion is a 'devil' after his life. This is part of the intricate webs of the battles in existence. In general terms, it is like praying for what to eat and at the same time praying against what will eat you.

ANNOTATION:
The eyes of a lion are on the goat; the eyes of the goat are on the grass. That is part of existence.

In this our Universe, there are diverse personalities and they have different kinds of food. We human beings have our food condiments as well. You make a farm and plant seeds, but you are not the manufacturer of the seeds which you plant. The Universal Spirit of the Almighty God assumes those forms you know as seed at lesser degrees. You plant rice; you plant coconut and eat; that is part of your food. One thing feeds on another thing. Everything you feed on in this world are creatures like you, just that you are higher than them in the scale of existence.

Likewise, there are also creatures far ahead of man in the universal scale of existence. Some of these higher beings feed on the energies arising from the mental animations of man's consciousness. (This point is well clarified in my book entitled **'Deeper Realities of Existence Vol. 1')**. When man causes pain to man and pain occurs in a particular environment, the psychic spheres of that pain, in conjunction with the vicious

ANNOTATION:
The book -- Deeper Realities of Existence -- is vital to the children of men. This is the hour to know more.

mental pattern of the perpetrator, generate energies in the mode of darkness. The mental energies thus generated coalesce into metaphysical animations that constitute 'food' to a particular kind of beings, namely, some forces of darkness.

To this end, it is important to know, in the light of eternal truth, for instance, that the pain which reverberates from the actions of rape, murder, war, terrorism, kidnapping, violence, robbery, amongst others, are the 'food' consumed by some vicious astral entities. The energies generated therein rises beyond the mundane aspects of the Earth's eco-systems generally known.

All of the energies arising from the human mental matrix, whether benevolent or malignant, have their invisible pathways in the subtle aspects of reality. Through these pathways, they travel into diverse levels and realms of realities beyond man.

ANNOTATION:
Man is an energy-essence compressed into a format that is gross material. Thus, he is a transmitting and receiving station of thoughts.

Now, when an energy generated from pain travels in this manner, it goes into the subjective systems of astral chambers of the forces of darkness.

Consequently, these forces hijack such energies and feed from them. Thus, they feed fat from the pain of the children of men. And from the point of view of these forces of darkness, their survival – in their terms of survival – solely depends on the practice of wickedness by the sons and daughters of men. Thus, for their survival in such terms, they fight day and night to ensure that wickedness thrives in the human realms of physical existence. They achieve this, however, via the constant invasion of the human minds, in proportion to the right they possess from the pool of probabilities earlier mentioned in the previous segment.

Furthermore, the earthman may be bamboozled in hearing that the divine qualities of love, peace, forgiveness, joy, justice, mercy, goodness, amongst

ANNOTATION:
Lust, anger, greed, vanity and attachment to the material things of life; these are channels of feeding the cosmic powers of the dark world.

others, also serve as 'food' to some higher personalities. These personalities, namely, some higher Forces of Light, are embellished within the framework of these divine qualities, which constitute their 'food'. They also feed fat from the human mental animations of the benevolent energies arising from the mode of goodness.

MAN AS FARMLAND

When we go beyond the physical systems of reality and have a glimpse into the ethereal environment of the universal metaphysical forces – Forces of Light and forces of darkness – you will recognize the essence of certain classifications in the hierarchy of entities not physically oriented. For instance, the ones that feed from the energy of our mental animation of wickedness, we classify as forces of darkness. The ones that feed from the energy that we generate through peace, love, mercy, joy, amongst others, we call the holy Angels– Forces of Light. God Himself in manifestations, within the ambit of

ANNOTATION:
Be useful for the divine network of the Forces of Light,
not for the vicious network of the most hideous astral entities.

His Eternal Light, isn't ruled out of this.

Consequently, some Forces of Light and forces of darkness are also entangled in the intricate webs of battles, as far as the cultivation of fruits of the farmland – the earthmen – is concerned. In general terms, however, the children of men are far from knowing this, nevertheless, it constitutes part of the mysteries of existence.

Now, I am not saying that all the forces of darkness fight to feed in the manner earlier stated, but that certain kind of the forces of darkness do so. And in this connection, I am speaking especially regarding some astral entities in the subtle realms of Earth and in some isolated portions of both the inner Space and the Solar System. Such entities feed from the vicious thoughts of humans. They also fight, as earlier stated, to ensure that their food is not exhausted; they invade the human minds, via the astral-waves, from time to time to generate the elements of wickedness that

ANNOTATION:
The art of feeding differs from creature to creature.
Swines may feed on human excreta, some humans feed on cow
meat, and certain astral entities do feed on humans.

constitute their food.

I write this letter to, amongst other things, warn you not to allow any power of darkness to feed from the thoughts of your heart. Do not yield to their devices. The main battles of life are within the consciousness of man. Only you and you alone can make the greatest efforts to be salvaged. Thus, Lord Buddha admonished the earthmen:

> ***"No one saves us but ourselves. No one can and no one may. We ourselves must walk the path Hatred does not***
>
> ***cease by hatred, but only by love; this is the eternal rule Suffering follows***
>
> ***an evil thought as the wheels of a cart follow the oxen that draws it".*** *(See the Buddhist holy book, The Tripitaka).*

ANNOTATION:
"Hatred does not cease by hatred, but only by love".
These words of Buddha holds the eternal validity of ascent in the
Light of God.

In the Holy Bible, Saint Paul questioned the earthmen in his admonition thus: **"Know ye not, that to whom ye yield yourselves servants to obey, his servants ye are to whom ye obey; whether of sin unto death, or of obedience unto righteousness?"**(Rom. 6:16; KJV). If we yield ourselves to sin – vicious mental pattern – we attract diverse deadly experiences to ourselves and our world. If we are situated in the mode of goodness – obedience to divine rules unto righteousness – we will form a sane world embedded in the practice of brotherhood of all existences.

Earthman, just know that as you are higher than smaller creatures – fowls, ants, lizards, cockroaches, rats and others – there are beings higher than you in the cosmic scale of existence. And there are mighty beings higher than what is higher than you, and so forth, in the unlimited cycle of evolvement unto the unlimited God. Therefore, know also that if you yield yourself to

ANNOTATION:
Yield yourself to what will uplift your life in the consciousness of the Holy Spirit, and not otherwise.

wickedness, then of course you will feed some forces of wickedness higher than you. But if you uphold the divine standards of Love, Peace, and Justice in mercy, you will equally attract the Forces of Light to help you in the journey of divine ascent.

Earthman, when you yield to the hosts of darkness and the forces of darkness come to you by their nature, don't expect them to behave like the Forces of Light. Haven't you read about the life and works of the Great Lord Jesus the Christ, Lord and Master of the Forces of Light? Compare it with the life and works of Adolf Hitler of Germany, who came to the physical world from a high den of darkness; then 'use your tongue to count your teeth'.

All creatures or beings in existence behave according to their predominant nature. Thus, lion will behave as lion and fowl will behave as fowl; also, man as man, woman as woman and child as child. The child will grow, but if the

ANNOTATION:
When a finger takes a dip into oil it affects the rest.
When you blame the hawk for stealing a chick you must scold the hen for playing in the open with her chicks.

child doesn't grow then there is a problem. And that is our problem. We, the earthmen, are like a child that has failed to grow. Sure, it is good to be a child, but it is not good to remain a child.

We have to allow ourselves to be useful in the farm or vineyard of the Light of God, because whatever uses you empowers you. If you are empowered by the forces of darkness, then be prepared to go down in the journey of life. However, if you stand firm on the platform of divine Light, then Light will add to Light and you will be empowered in Light; and Light will overcome darkness for you.

There are certain dimensions of forces in the Universe that are capable of using humans, within the earthly camouflage systems, as 'toys'. These include both the Forces of Light and the forces of darkness. And the dimension you yield yourself to, is of utmost importance in this regard. The Forces of Light do not use man

ANNOTATION:
Born as a child, the earthman has refused to grow in divine terms.
He who fails to wake up cannot stand.

as 'toy' – using man against man – even though they have the capacity to do so, but the forces of darkness do.

The forces of darkness use the children of men that yield to them as toys. Such earthmen are mere marionettes in their terms, and this is very dangerous to Soul personalities in the human embodiment. The earthmen seen and used as marionettes by the forces of darkness, are people that are captured in the first place by them.

The marionettes are captured and used to capture more earthmen, in the vicious cycle of astral manipulations. They are completely in the mode of darkness, taking great pleasure in the pains and sufferings of fellow earthmen. When you hear about people killing other people, through wars, armed robbery, terrorists attack, raping women, kidnapping, arsonists on rampage and other forms of wickedness, we condemn the perpetrators. However, we

ANNOTATION:
Mundane religion is like a toy in the hands of a child.
If you force the toy out of the hands of a child, the child will cry.

condemn them, but that is in the human terms; and this does not contribute to anything meaningful. In the divine terms, we should be praying for the spiritual transformation of such earthly marionettes. Such earthmen are captured and used by forces far more than them. Praying for their transformations is our major contribution to the universal pool of probabilities, from whence comes the right of divine intervention by the Forces of Light in the affairs of men. We will make this more clearer in subsequent segments of this material.

BEAR FRUITS IN YOUR FARM

There are constant extraterrestrial battles in the Space – Space combats – related to the foregoing expositions. Though in specific divine reality, Space is illusion and does not exist from the basic nature and point of view of extraterrestrials. Such higher Intelligences do not see what we know as 'Space' ultimately within the

ANNOTATION:
While claiming innocent, we aid diverse wickedness in our world,
through our vicious thought projections

framework of human perceptions. But from the human perception, there is nothing to qualify such reality other than 'Space'.

There are constant battles, as earlier mentioned, going on in what we know as 'Space', between the Forces of Light and forces of darkness, some of which are connected and related to the world of man. In some higher dimensions of forces, whether of Light or darkness, as earlier stated, the Earth-world is considered a 'farmland'. And in such terms, the earthmen are seen as farm products.

Now, as you read this material, ask yourself: 'Who is farming on me?' And say to yourself: 'I don't want the forces of darkness to farm and feed on me'. Resolve to stand firm on this, and contribute to salvaging our world. Resolve to be a farmland of the Lord in His Spirit of Light, so that you will bear the fruits of righteousness. And, surely, you will be the first beneficiary of this in the

ANNOTATION:
Space combat is a primordial art of hidden warfare. Remember the 'Prince of Persia' in the Holy Bible.

journey of life, here and hereafter. The manifestation of God we know as the Great Lord Jesus the Christ spoke to the faithful earthmen thus:

> *"I am the true vine, and my Father is the husbandman. Every branch in me that beareth not fruit He taketh away: and every branch that beareth fruit, he purgeth it, that it may bring forth more fruit ... I am the vine, ye are the branches: He that abideth in me, and I in him, the same bringeth forth much fruit: for without me ye can do nothing"* *(Jn. 15:1,2,5; KJV).*

There is a powerful Christian morning devotional song, which goes thus: **"Early in the morning, our Father God goes to His farm".**

ANNOTATION:
You are here to bear fruits -- the fruits of righteousness or the fruits of wickedness -- the choice is yours. But you must inherit the rewards of your fruits.

When you hear that the earthmen are referred to as a 'farmland' of God, we must be spiritually wise enough to be glad therein and bear good fruits in the mode of goodness.

The Extraterrestrial Intelligence (Angel of Light) that spoke to the great Prophet Moses, told him that **"The LORD God planted a garden eastward in Eden; and there He put the man whom He had formed"** (Gen. 2:7; KJV). That is the biblical account of the descent of man into the physical realms of Earth. Thus, man is likened to a seed planted in a garden or farm. And the seed is expected to grow and bear good fruits in the Light of God.

What are these good fruits? They are summarised and embedded in Love, Peace and Justice in mercy. God Himself partakes in these fruits. In some instances, the Holy Bible refers to the Lord both as 'Husbandman' and a Husband celebrating marriage. (See Jn. 15:1 and Rev. 19:7--9). And it is written: **"The husbandman**

ANNOTATION:
Early in the morning, our Father God goes to His farm.
We are that farm.

that laboureth must be first partaker of the fruits" (2 Tim. 2:6; KJV).

The fruits of our tongues are also important here. The wise king Solomon said: **"Death and life are in the power of the tongue: and they that love it shall eat the fruit thereof"** (Pro. 18:21; KJV). And on where the fruits of wickedness are domiciled in the demonic realms, God spoke through Prophet Isaiah thus:

> *"Rejoice not thou, whole Palestina, because the rod of him that smote thee is broken: for out of the serpent's root shall come forth a cockatrice, and his fruit shall be a fiery flying serpent"* (Isa. 14:29; KJV).

The Great Lord Jesus the Christ admonished us thus: **"Behold, I send you forth as sheep in the**

midst of wolves: be ye therefore wise as serpents, and harmless as doves" (Math. 10:16; KJV). The fruits of Love, Peace and Justice in mercy, are produced in the mode of goodness under the platform of divine wisdom. We must be spiritually wise to subjugate the manipulations of demons. The wise ones in the world of man, who have risen in the Light of God in this connection, are very dear to the One Eternal Almighty God. To this end, God spoke in the ancient Bhagavad Gita thus:

> *"The evil-doers and the deluded, who are the lowest of men, do not seek Me; they whose knowledge is destroyed by illusion follow the ways of demons .... The wise, ever steadfast and devoted to the One, excels; for, I am exceedingly dear to the wise and he is dear to Me .... I deem the wise man as My very*

ANNOTATION:
"Fiery flying serpent", which men see not, yet is beyond the veil; a high den of the forces of darkness.

Self; for, steadfast in mind, he is established in Me alone as the supreme goal" (Bhag. G. 7:15,17,18).

Earthmen, the foregoing subject is to guide us towards the recognition that we are the 'farmland' of God in certain terms. So, it is better for the Spirit of the Lord to harvest from us in the Light of God. Let God farm on us and bring out the fruit of life in goodness, the fruit of righteousness, the fruit of peace, the fruit of joy, amongst others. And whatever the Lord does with these fruits will surely give the holy Angels the right to come and intervene in our world.

People sometimes cry thus to God: 'Oh Lord come and intervene in my life'. For God to intervene in your life or in the world of man, there must be basis for such intervention; the right of intervention must be established. That is why sometimes when problem comes, the earthman is directed to fast and pray to God for

ANNOTATION:
Our steadfastness in the mode of goodness brings us closer to the Throne of Light in the Heavenly realms of God.

solution. This, when done in the proper perspective of divine Light, enables the pre-dominating propensity of the coarse energy of the body to step down, for the Spirit of God to rise and intervene.

The Spirit of God will intervene only in the life of a person who has a reference point for such intervention. This kind of exposition is to notify the earthman that some forces do feed from the mental energies of humans. As you are reading this material now, you can't escape the vast connectivity of thoughts in this regard. Here, even your slightest thought is involved. Whatever you think in your mind are projected through either the positive or negative poles of the mental matrix, via the invisible pathways, to the realms of Light or the chambers of darkness.

The energy of each thought goes beyond the three dimensional worlds. The physical realms of Earth are amongst the realms that belong

ANNOTATION:
Though we are currently situated in the realms of Matter, Energy, Space and Time (MEST), what proceeds from us transcends the gestalt of MEST.

to the three dimensional worlds of Matter, Energy, Space and Time (MEST). Thoughts ultimately go beyond the realms, rudiments and frameworks of MEST. In such terms, thoughts become the impetus of seeding other realities, in a manner generally unknown to the earthmen.

In the future, our science will be truly advanced to the point of having a 'soul', because what we have now is a 'soul-less science', in extraterrestrial terms. In the future, our science will advance and meet with religion at the point of universal threshold. Then the earthman will come to the point of knowing that, his thoughts are not only beyond the three dimensional realities, but they form matter in a gigantic endeavour.

Now, if the earthman is told that, in the light of eternal truth, his thoughts form matter, as well as some catastrophic natural events, he may be bamboozled. He doesn't know at the

ANNOTATION:
*'Soul-less' science is bereft of the validity of the divine spheres of reality. It is devoid of the recognition of the spiritual aspects of reality. **Its focus is on the material aspects of things.***

moment that his vicious thoughts, at certain levels of mass intensity, do coalesce into matter. Neither does he know that things like ocean mega-waves, meteoric invasions, earthquakes, volcanic eruptions, amongst others, can be physically manifested arising from some collective aspects of man's vicious mental pattern. Our sciences and religions haven't gotten to that point of knowing, yet it is part of the reality of existence, as communicated by Extraterrestrial Intelligences beyond humans.

So, what we are saying is that this is the time for us to take a firm stand on the path of Light and bear the fruits of Love, Peace and Justice in mercy for all. We must take a stand now to be saved from ourselves. If you are in a hole and you want to be helped, please first bring out your hands from the hole. Don't just stay there without bringing out your hands and expect someone to help you out. Bring out your hands first and a helper will come.

ANNOTATION:

The dimensions of most Extraterrestrial Intelligences, more vivid and valid than the world of man, lie millions and billions of years ahead of the world of man.

Therefore, make a move towards the Light of God; take a step towards goodness in the Light of the Almighty, and the holy Ones above will help you. Greater aspects of the subtle realities of universal existence are well structured in a highly complicated manner. Nevertheless, he who is situated in the mode of goodness, regardless of the complexity of universal realities, will surely excel in the universal scale of existence.

God bless the reader.

ANNOTATION:
Take a sincere step towards God and, surely, God will take several steps towards you.

DANGEROUS HOUR

Dear reader, Peace be with you. Few days ago, a higher Intelligence from the realms of Light above visited the **Harbinger of the Last Covenant**. It was a scheduled visit, of

ANNOTATION:
Beware, we have finally come to the hour of the long foretold end-time. The world will be bamboozled by the events that will come to pass.

which I was informed four days before then. He disclosed many things to me, some of which are not connected with the subject matter of this material.

Amongst the things he mentioned is a particular battle raging now in the astral realms of Earth, related to two major things used by the most vicious astral entities in battle now against the world of man. These are (i) anger and (ii) lack of forgiveness. Some forces of darkness are hanging on these two things, arising from the children of men, in their attempts to destroy us.

However, some units of the Forces of Light, under the divine authority of the **King of Kings and Lord of Lords**, are sent into some astral chambers of darkness to fight and defuse the enormous vicious energy accumulated by the forces of darkness in this regard. It is not an easy battle, as no battle is easy. Moreover, as

ANNOTATION:
Anger and lack of forgiveness: avoid these by all means now, as much as you can. Many will be ruined within the ambit of these.

we continue to generate anger and unforgiving mental patterns, we will continue to empower the hosts of darkness against ourselves.

We, the children of men, have caused a lot of havoc in our families, communities and nations through anger and unforgiving heart. All forms of violence are the manifestations of anger; and all forms of revenge and reprisals are products of lack of forgiveness. But in the formation of a new world of divine Light, already in the making, these won't be allowed to dominate, as it is at the moment. The battles to achieve this, is ongoing, and no matter how long it takes in the human terms, victory will hopefully be enacted.

However, be warned that this is a very dangerous time for anyone to live in anger and unforgiving heart. In these now – **anger and unforgiving heart** – you will surely attract many unpleasant situations around yourself, even faster than ever. The only solution is for us to uphold the consciousness of Love, Peace and Justice in mercy at all times. But remember, Love, Peace and Justice in mercy must first inhabit your consciousness before you will begin to express them.

DON'T ADD SALT TO INJURY

Dear people of Planet Earth, the Peace that brings true Justice in Love and mercy, is absolutely imperative in the world of man today than ever. For ages we, the sons and daughters of men, have conducted the experiments of our physical existence and experience mostly under the predominance of violence. And of violence, this has debased mankind in so many ways, thereby necessitating the need for us to be saved from ourselves.

In Nigeria, for instance, violence and insecurity, which are generated by lack of Love, Peace and Justice in diverse quarters, are evidently great impediments to progress and development.

ANNOTATION:
The experiment that will salvage us must be based, not on hate, but on love, peace and justice in mercy for all.

This is so in other parts of the world, whether in This the developed or the developing nations. We are so violent that we don't even have value for human life anymore. We do to others what we wouldn't want others to do to us, contrary to divine injunctions and admonitions. The Lord Himself warned:

> **"Therefore all things whatsoever ye would that men should do to you, do ye even so to them: for this is the law and the prophets" (Math. 7:12; KJV).**

This is the hour for each and everyone of us, from within the rudiments of our inner selves, our mental patterns and mind- sets, to compliment any genuine effort of government towards Peace. But we must do this on a higher divine platform, from our heart of hearts. No genuine effort towards peace is irrelevant, no matter how little it is.

ANNOTATION:
You kill fellow earthman, but you don't want to be killed; be warned because you will never escape the Universal Law of Reciprocal Action.

Consistent daily prayers, for the Holy Spirit to transform the core agents of hate, who coordinate and spread violence and insecurity in our world, are extremely important now than ever. All efforts towards the genuine transformation of these agents of darkness are needed now than ever.

This must not be taken lightly, individually and collectively, if we must be salvaged from ourselves. We must know that something divine must be done on Earth for the intervention of the higher Heavenly realms of Light. The Holy Spirit needs our sincere prayers of Love in this connection, for the intervention of great Intelligences (Angels of Light) above. There are Angelic Ones above, who are divinely empowered by the Lord to help us. However, we must grant them the right to help us to subjugate the vicious spirits of the agents of darkness in our midst.

These agents of hate, spreading insecurity and violence in our world, are our brothers and

ANNOTATION:
Contribute your energy -- your prayers -- to the transformation of the vicious minded humans. Surely, you are the first beneficiary of this by divine laws.

sisters of the human family. They are mere marionettes and captives of powerful forces of darkness far beyond them, especially the vicious forces of the astral realms of Earth. They equally need our help.

Our foremost duty now is to continue to pray for their transformations in love. We must not hate them or channel any emotion of hatred towards them. Doing so will be like adding salt to injury, in accordance with the inexorable Universal Law of Reciprocal Action.

BE COMMITTED TO HELPING THE WEAK

These agents of darkness are already embedded with the weakest part of human existence, namely, hate. The vicious astral entities, by their nature, need these agents daily. They need them for the increase of their 'farm'; the increase of the energy arising from violence and sustaining the kind of 'food' they eat. Hating these human agents of darkness, places us on the same

ANNOTATION:
Lord Buddha said: "If men hate you, regard it not; and you can
turn the hate of men to love and mercy and goodwill, and mercy is
as large as all the heavens" (Aq-G. 11:6).

platform from which the forces of darkness operate. And no solution from above comes in this system. Love, Peace and Justice in mercy are the only keys that we have in God.

Consequently, we can't help them overcome what holds them down, and we can't help ourselves overcome what they do, nor receive the help from above, for as long as we are on the same platform, the same page of hate, with them. The Spirit of the Lord used the **Harbinger of the Last Covenant** to give a holy book of 518 pages to the earthmen of our time, as was given to me from above, entitled **'Verses of Eternal Truth'**. From the onset of that book, I spoke against this kind of experience thus:

> *"... Therefore I say: organise your entire life, in your thoughts, words and deeds, from the point of fearlessness Let this fearlessness be embedded in the framework of selfless*

ANNOTATION:

The Great Lord Jesus the Christ taught us to pray thus: "Forgive us our debts, as we forgive our debtors" (Math. 6:12). Whoever fails to uphold this, plunges downward in the journey of life.

Divine Love, and let this selfless Divine Love again be embedded with the knowledge of your core spiritual multidimensional identity; and of this knowledge, let it rise in the essence of the Divine authority of the Lord, who leads on the path of Light.

"It is only then, Oh earthman, that you will be strong to truly guide and help your fellow humans, who organise their lives from the point of fear, from the point of hate, from the point of ignorance of the true nature of existence.

"When life is organised from the point of fear, man becomes subjugated to darkness in the

ANNOTATION:
The masterminds have said that fear is an illusion by which one rides faster into the chambers of the dead. Live in love, not in fear.

journey of life. And this path is the sinking sand. Help those that are sinking to rise, but you must first be strong in the Lord.

"If one standing on a mud is sinking therein and you want to help him out, how would you go about it? If you stand on the same platform with him, upon the sinking mud, to help him, I tell you, both of you will sink together. Will a sinking man thank you who has gone to help him out on the same platform in which both of you are sinking?

"No one sinking will appreciate another sinking along with him. Therefore, stand your feet upon a solid ground, even upon the rock, then you can help those sinking to rise " (VOET. 1:1—6).

ATTRACTING PEACE OR WICKEDNESS

Earthmen, let it be known that the inexorable Universal Law of Reciprocal Action, which is immutable, works in all facets of the entire Universal Systems. As earlier stated, this Universal Law is implemented in the entire Universal Systems, by the manifestations of God we know as the **Supreme Lords of Justice and Retribution.**

The immutable Universal Law of Reciprocal Action plays out on the physical realms of Earth, especially in the life of a person or persons. It plays out in all facets of being. It plays out in all fabrics of the certainty of consciousness, which includes but not limited to the emotional energy. It plays out in conjunction with the inexorable Universal Law of Homogeneity. As it plays

ANNOTATION:
Consciousness is the basis of certainty, whilst certainty is the primordial offshoot of the Universal Laws embedded in the Seed-Giving-Father of all existences and realities.

out, we attract to ourselves, amongst other things, the intense objects of our emotions.

Thus, in this terms, therefore, a nation that loves Peace will attract Peace and experience Peace. A nation that hates war, however, will not attract nor experience Peace. In the human terms of understanding, this is a paradox that may be perceived as contradicting itself.

Nevertheless, in the divine spheres of reality, transcending the physical aspects generally known, which strictly follow the rudiments of the inexorable Universal Laws of the One Eternal Almighty God, there are no contradictions in the foregoing expressions. This will be clarified as we continue.

Simply put: we, individually and collectively, attract into the awareness of our life experiences the dearest intense mental and subtle focus of our emotions. All emotions are primarily

ANNOTATION:
Paradoxes constitute the fundamental basis of the deeper mysteries of being.

governed by love and hate. Peace and Justice, encapsulating mercy and joy, are fundamental prime and primordial offshoots of the emotions of Love. Anger, quarrel and all sorts of fighting, killing and maiming, are also the fundamental prime and primordial offshoots of the emotions of hate.

As earlier expressed, we attract to ourselves, into our consciousness and experiences, the elements and objects of our emotions. In other words, the earthman attracts to himself, via the gradations and intensities of his emotional energy, what he loves most and, unfortunately, what he hates as well. This is strictly in accordance with the inexorable Universal Laws, working within the ambit of the gestalt of three subjective principles of being, namely:

(i)   Expectation,

(ii) Wish and

(iii) Desire.

ANNOTATION:
All manifestations are premised on expectation, wish and desire.

All these are interrelated and embedded within the framework of emotions, as a rule. It should be known that expectation, wish and desire rule all actions in all the Universes of God. The actions of God Himself and His diverse direct multitudinous manifestations in the Universes, are premised on expectation, wish and desire.

Furthermore, the actions of Extraterrestrial Intelligences (Angelic Beings) in the higher realms of either Light or darkness, are embedded within these. The actions of humanoids in all the Planetary Systems, the children of men, amongst others, follow both the flexibility and mobility of the aforementioned principles of expectation, wish and desire.

Now, the emotional energy must be discharged whenever any of these principles plays out, at varying range of intensities. These intensities are enacted on and absorbed by homogenous entities and realities, following the Universal

ANNOTATION:
All interrelated consciousness have a 'day in God', and that 'day', in our terms, is eternal.

Laws. And whilst Love which generates Peace and Justice, as well as hate which generates fighting and killings, are the foremost propensities of emotions, we therefore attract both what we love and what we hate.

The emotion of love is embedded within the subtle aspects of the psyche chromosomes of the normal mind faculties, namely, the four fundamental faculties of the mind. (For details on this, see my book entitled '**Mind Rudiments vol. 1'**). Also, the emotion of hate comes forth from the fifth abnormal faculty of the mind, which gives birth to its five deadly propensities, namely, lust, anger, greed, vanity and attachment to the material things of the earth-life.

Thus, our mental patterns, feelings and thoughts are mostly absorbed in the objects of our love-focus, in which our minds are at peace with. The emotional energy of such feelings and thoughts attracts the object of our love to us, in

ANNOTATION:
The rigidity of mental stances is devoid of the mobility and flexibility required for the excellence of consciousness on the way to God.

accordance with the inexorable Universal Law of Homogeneity. In this vein, you have Peace and Justice when you love Peace and Justice. Thus, a nation that loves Peace will experience Peace; a person who loves Peace will experience same.

Conversely, our mental patterns, feelings and thoughts are also absorbed in the object of our hate, in order to constantly uphold within our consciousness that such is truly hated by us. When you hate a person or a thing, you also often think of such a person or thing that you hate. The cogitations along this line, your thoughts therein, also follow the recognition and subtle realities of homogeneity, by virtue of the Universal Laws that govern existence.

Consequently, you will attract to yourself the object of your hate, via the intensity of your emotional focus. In this vein, you experience hate when you accommodate the elements of hate and its attendant consequences of wickedness

ANNOTATION:

By virtue of the Universal Law of Homogeneity, in accordance with the rudiments of emotional discharge, we attract into the fabrics of our experiences the intense focus of our emotions, whether love or hate.

in your emotions. As such, a nation that hates war will not experience peace. Hope the point is clear to some extent.

THE MAIN PROBLEM

It must be understood here that the emotion of hate is the main problem. All emotions, whether of love or hate, go with feelings and thought intensities. At certain range of intensities, the emotional energy, via thoughts and feelings, whether expressed individually or within the subtle ambit of mass production, coalesce into a subjective framework that serve as the impetus to other realities.

When thoughts and feelings coalesce into other realities, they initiate the formation of tentacles that are finally transmogrified to both matter and events. This is part of the mysteries of existence. The aspects of the transmogrification of thoughts and feelings into matter, are generally unknown to the religions and sciences of the Earth-world. This recognition lies within the

ANNOTATION:
When our thoughts reach certain dimensions, they become what the earthman cannot comprehend at this moment of the earth-life.

purview of Extraterrestrial Intelligences (Forces of Light or Angelic Beings) in the Heavenly realms of Light.

However, the transformation of thoughts and feelings into events, are to some extent known to the earthmen in relative, not absolute, terms. This is because such knowledge is not generally pursued in the world of man, as it should, in our diverse fields of studies. Yet, this is fundamental in all aspects of human existence and experience.

For instance, we are battling with insecurity today in Nigeria and other parts of the world. We blame, hate and cast aspersions on the multitudinous elements of insecurity, masters of terrorism and agents of darkness in our world. By so doing, whether or not we know it, following specific related Universal Laws, we contribute our energies into the pool of probabilities, via the Universal Law of the Probable Systems, against ourselves.

ANNOTATION:
The hour is coming when the knowledge of the earthman will expand tremendously, rising beyond the coordinating ego of physical experience, into intercepting and absorbing hidden truths that are part of his whole self.

It is from this pool of probabilities that the energies of vicious thoughts physically oriented are transmitted to diverse vicious minds on the physical realms of Earth. The sons and daughters of men absorb these energies via the process of mind invasion. This process is guided by the vicious astral entities, consequent upon the subtle right that they receive from the pool of probabilities. And the humans whose minds are thus invaded, swing into the acts of wickedness in the guise of belief systems, joblessness, revenge, amongst other factors. They physically enact all sorts of repugnant behaviours within these framework, namely, the mode of darkness.

We must understand that portions of the energies, arising from our individual and collective mental patterns and mind- sets of hate towards wicked people, are filtered in the subtle pool of probabilities. These are absorbed by the most hedonistic and vicious forces of the astral realms.

ANNOTATION:
Whatever you hold as the motivating basis of following the path of criminality and wickedness, is the end result of the subtle invasion of your mind by the vicious astral entities.

These vicious astral entities empower the vicious minds on the physical realms of Earth, in the perpetration of all sorts of wickedness in the world of man. Thus, in such terms, we, the children of men, contribute in all these things, unknown to us. We contribute, individually and collectively, to all kinds of wicked practices on Earth, through our individual and collective wrong primordial mental stances, mental patterns, bereft of true Love, Peace and Justice in mercy.

God bless the reader.

ANNOTATION:
Empowerment is part of the offshoot of existence; but, in this case, it depends on what is empowering you, whether the Spirit of God in Light or spirits of the dark world.

ABANDONING OURSELVES TO OURSELVES

Dear people of Planet Earth, in all the generations of the children of men, the masterminds on Earth have admonished us on the need for peaceful co-existence. Great Extraterrestrial Intelligences of Light in the higher Planetary Systems beyond the world of man, have often sent messages telling us to ensure that we live in Love, maintain Peace, uphold Justice and show Mercy in the world of man.

Even the Lord of the Universe Himself, in His manifestations at diverse times in diverse places, has warned the earthmen about the danger of not following the path of peaceful co- existence. The divine message of the Lord to man is always directed to the point of the earthmen upholding Love, Peace and Justice in all our affairs on Earth.

The Holy Ones from above, Extraterrestrial Intelligences in divine Light, are seriously concerned about where the earthmen have placed themselves through the existence based on violence and hate. These great Ones from above have assiduously warned us, the children of

ANNOTATION:
Never discard any admonition geared towards the peaceful co-existence of humans in the world of man.

men, about the consequences of abandoning ourselves solely to ourselves on the path of hate. This is disastrous, as presently seen in our world.

To this end, we have it on record that a certain Extraterrestrial Intelligence (great Angelic Being of Light) resident in another Planet, a great personality not physically oriented, (names withheld) sent a message in our time to the Earth-world and to the children of men thus: **"If you abandon yourselves to yourselves, then what good would seem to spring out of the heavens of your being?"** Speaking further to the people of this world, this Intelligence said:

> *"Your world is not in dire straits because you trust yourselves, but because you do not. Your social institutions are set up to fence in the individual, rather than to allow the natural development of the individual ....You must honour*

ANNOTATION:
He who abandons himself to himself on the vicious path of destruction, is like a man inside a pit who has refused to lift up his hand for help.

yourselves and see within yourselves the Spirit of eternal validity. You must honour all other individuals, because within each is the spark of this validity".

PATH OF DIVINE ASCENT

As earlier stated, Extraterrestrial Intelligences or Angelic Beings from diverse higher Heavenly realms of Light, have been communicating with the Earth-world from time to time, via diverse channels. These have engaged themselves towards admonishing the earthmen on the path of divine ascent. They are willing to help the earthmen, within the limit of the right they have to intervene.

The path of divine ascent guides us to be what we were made to be, and not otherwise. The path of divine ascent leads us via the consciousness of

ANNOTATION:
Endeavour to honour all men, whether or not they honour you, and the honour from above will speak for you at last.

practical demonstration of Love and Peace. This is the sacred path wherein lies the framework of Divine Justice. This path is completely embedded with the consciousness and the practical application of the brotherhood of all existences, all realities.

This is absolutely necessary if we, the children of men, must be saved from ourselves. The masterminds and the Lord Himself, all have warned that we must not return to the vicious old path of our forefathers, embedded with the aggrandizement of killing and maiming fellow earthmen, in the misguided belief systems of fighting for God or for the gods.

We subjugate Love, Peace and Justice on Earth in the quest to acquire fame, money, high office, land, property and other mundane things. The insatiable quest for these things, is to our perils. And the fact remains that these things are left behind when one finally leaves the physical realms of Earth and face other realities, through the experience we know as death.

ANNOTATION:
Divine ascent is the upward journey of Souls in the first resting point of destination. The encumbrances inherent in your delay to rise to this point, is your own making.

THE VICIOUS OLD PATH

We must strive to abolish in our psyche and belief systems the mental stances of our forefathers, bereft of peaceful co- existence. We must strive, individually and collectively, to imbibe the consciousness of the brotherhood of all existences, whether or not our forefathers lived in that system.

In specific terms, the vicious old path can only enhance the subjugation of the human race. It is said that **'a wise child will kill what killed his father, but a foolish child will be killed by what killed his father'**. To this end, the aforementioned Extraterrestrial Intelligence further warned the earthmen thus:

> *"Do not fall into the old ways that will lead you precisely into the world that you fear.*

ANNOTATION:
The old vicious path of our forefathers didn't grant us excellence on the path of Light, wherein lies peaceful co-existence. We must be wise enough not to continue therein.

"There is no man who hates but that hatred is reflected outward and made physical, and there is no man who loves but that love is reflected outward and made physical. The human race is in a stage through which various forms of consciousness travel.

"Your world (Earth) is a training system for emerging consciousness. In your world, you must first learn to handle energy and see through physical materialisation, the concrete result of thought and emotion".

Distinguished people of Planet Earth, let it be emphasized that Peace and Justice proceed from the divine fountain of the practical application of Love. Without Love there will be no Peace

ANNOTATION:
The physical realms of Earth is a training camp for certain kinds of Souls in our Solar System. Peace and love guide us to pass the exams in the school of the earth-life

and Justice. And without Peace and Justice, progress can't be made by anyone in the journey of life in divine terms.

THE BLESSED ONES

In our time, another Extraterrestrial Intelligence of a high divine dimension spoke. This great One dwells in the hidden aspects of the realm of "morning Stars" (Job 38:7). This is a Heavenly realm of Light located in the transcendental fabrics of the Venus Planet. He (names withheld) did transmit a message to the Earth-world at one time related to the blessings of God on the workers of Peace on Earth. Part of this highly revered divine message reads thus:

> *"In this times of unrest in your world (Earth), the workers for Peace are indeed thrice blessed. For these ones, by their toil, sacrifice their own bliss. By their interest in*

ANNOTATION:
The hierarchy of interplanetary confederation of the Extraterrestrial Forces of Light in our Solar System, is referred to as the meeting of 'God and the Sons of God' in the Bible'. (See Job 38:7; 1:6; 1 Kings 22:19--22).

the suffering of their brothers they sacrifice their peace. Blessed are these ones at this time.

"Their handiwork will increase and their monuments, built upon sure foundation, will last so that the future generations may look in reverence upon these.

"Thrice blessed in the Now – and by Now – are these ones, for they have demonstrated unselfishness in the most definite holy way. This strange world (Earth) needs the guiding hands of these ones and they give their hands to the strangers in the wilderness of materialism".

ANNOTATION:
When we say that the earthman must be saved from himself, it also means that he must be saved from the wilderness of materialism, the real dungeon of the earth-life.

In another occasion, a divine message from the Almighty God, in His Versions manifested as the 'Supreme Lords', was given to the earthmen. This was done via an Extraterrestrial Intelligence resident in a Heavenly realm of Light. This Heavenly realm is located in the subtle aspects of the Mars Planet. And the Intelligence himself (Archangel) is a high ranking divine official in the universal hierarchy of the 'Cosmic Brotherhood of Space Masters'. The divine message admonished the earthmen thus:

"Love is not the result of ignorance, but the direct result of applied enlightenment. Become enlightened, gain understanding of the feelings and problems of all peoples and Love becomes a living, vibrant, all-pervasive thing.

ANNOTATION:
The Cosmic Brotherhood of Space Masters is a highly divinely empowered extraterrestrial squad of the Forces of Light within and beyond our Solar System, well represented in the interplanetary confederation.

> ***"In our observations of Earth, we have noted that the slayer of Love is hypocrisy. Many, content in their procrastinations, hypocritically talk and bandy this word about, till it hath no meaning, save a vague, misunderstood academic one".***

As earlier said, Peace comes from Love and Love must be practically demonstrated through Justice and selfless service to God and man. By these, our deeds are validated in the divine spheres of the Almighty God.

ESSENCE OF DIVINE SERVICE

Divine service to others, with the heart of Love in God- consciousness, is prerequisite for peaceful co-existence of humans. This is the foundation of Light of the New World – the Paradise we seek on Earth. The Kingdom of God on Earth is predicated on this platform of divine service. The same Intelligence (Archangel) from Mars, speaking as received from the 'Supreme Lords', further said:

> *"If you would, at this very moment, begin to build tomorrow's temple upon the sure foundation of today's right action, you would serve.*
>
> *"If you would be free from the materialistic prison cunningly devised to enslave you, you would serve If you would prepare yourselves for the New World, you would serve.*
>
> *".... Break away from your own troubles by concentrating upon the sufferings of others. Serve in the*

ANNOTATION:
The new world of love, peace and justice in mercy is already in the making.
Its foundation is on the practical realisation of the brotherhood of all existences.

great spiritual battle and you can walk with head high and stand in any Hall unafraid to read what be written there.

".... By Your service, you can throw a dazzling beam of scintillating white vibrant energy into the darkness of a suffering world – and raise it. It is – by God it is – the Jewel in the Rock of Attainment".

Ladies and gentlemen of our world, selfless service of Love to fellow earthmen in the Name of God, is the 'mother' of Peace and peaceful co-existence of the human family. It is equally the 'father' of Justice in mercy, in the world of man.

ANNOTATION:
He who seeks for divine help should first help others with what he has. Selfishness will exert upon the earthman the pressures of darkness.

Again, it is the panacea to all forms of terrorism and wickedness on the physical realms of Earth. Without it, all other efforts, especially by the use of arms, towards abating terrorism and all forms of wickedness, won't work.

God bless the reader.

ANNOTATION:

Using the force of arms to enforce peace, will never usher in the needed peace that has eluded the Earth-world for ages.

ENERGY OF PEACE IN LOVE

Dear people of Planet Earth, some of you may be aware that in the Christian Holy Bible, the word 'Peace' has 399 matching words. Some of these words were spoken by the Lord Himself, while some were spoken by other masterminds inspired by the Spirit of the Lord.

For instance, the wise King Solomon expressed how joyful existence emanates from Peace. In his words: **"To the counsellors of peace is joy"** (Pro. 12:20; KJV). Of course, without Peace in the life of a person or group of persons, joy is absent. Again, a wise one, Eliphaz the Temanite, said: **"Acquaint now thyself with Him, and be at peace: thereby good shall come unto thee"** (Job 22:21; KJV).

Here, we learn that the goodness of existence flourishes in the midst of those who maintain the consciousness of Peace with fellow men, and the Almighty, the **Seed-Giving-Father** of all realities. The evidence of this, however, is peaceful co- existence of all humans.

Thus, Saint Paul admonished: **"If it be possible, as much as lieth in you, live peaceably with**

ANNOTATION:
The destroyers of the human race should be warned: they will be destroyed in the hands of what uses them.

all men" (Rom. 12:18; KJV). He also clarified that the vicious minded earthmen are ignorant of the essence of peaceful co-existence of the human family. In his words:

> ***"Their feet are swift to shed blood: Destruction and misery are in their ways: And the way of peace have they not known. There is no fear of God before their eyes"*** *(Rom. 3:15—18; KJV).*

The haters and destroyers of the human family have no value for Justice and peaceful co-existence of the earthmen; they do not know the way to Peace. It is the bona-fide duty of the lovers of Peace and Justice to teach them the ways of Peace. And to achieve this, we must begin with the process of sending them daily thought-energy of Peace and Love in our prayers, mental patterns and meditations.

ANNOTATION:
The debt we owe in the Universe is paid by ensuring that we send our daily prayers of divine transformation to the vicious minded earthmen.

BE SPIRITUALLY MINDED

We can't do this if we ourselves are not spiritually minded. Spiritual mindedness entails true divine enlightenment on the path of Light. Mundane attachments and carnal mindedness will inhibit us from making any meaningful progress on the path of Peace. Thus, Saint Paul further warned: **"For to be carnally minded is death; but to be spiritually minded is life and peace"** (Rom. 8:6; KJV).

When we merely speak of Peace, whilst our secret thoughts dovetail with the inner consciousness of hate, acrimony, injustice and dichotomy, our actions will certainly show evidence of wickedness to fellow earthmen. This enhances the spread of wickedness in our world, from the hidden dimensions generally unknown to the earthmen.

In Homer's 'The Iliad', this is spoken of in this manner: **"Hateful to me as the gates of Hades**

ANNOTATION:
When we have undue attachment to the material things of life, we are seen as 'dead men' in the divine spheres of reality.

is the man who hides one thing in his heart and speaks another". This consciousness, especially when the inner heart is fixed on hate, is a major contribution to the network of darkness fighting this world. All of us are involved in this aspect of battle even on a daily basis. We all need inward purity to scale through.

This inward purity of heart, the experience thereof, was part of the prayers offered to God by Socrates, wisest man of his time. In 'The Dialogues of Plato', Socrates prayed thus: **"I pray Thee, O God, that I may be beautiful within".** Socrates admonished the earthman to endeavour to be kind to his fellow earthmen, as we are all involved in the battles of life.

In his words: **"Be kind, for everyone you meet is fighting a hard battle".** Part of the battles of life is the battle to uphold the existence of Peace and Justice in Love. This can't be achieved by the force of arms, but by eradicating hate and wickedness in the hearts of men.

ANNOTATION:
Inward purity of heart gives birth to genuine love, peace and justice in mercy for all in the world of man.

WORK HARD IN SILENCE

When we achieve Peace in Love within us, it will flow outward for peaceful co-existence in the world of man. Consequently, our efforts to this end should be mostly enacted in the silent aspects of being. As we endeavour at all times to imbibe the consciousness of Peace within the silent and secret recesses of our hearts, our success will be outwardly materialized to the sanity of existence on the physical realms of Earth. As said by the wise ones of old, **'work hard in silence, let your success be your noise'**.

Socrates also prayed thus: **"Give me beauty in the inward Soul; may the outward and the inward be at one"**. He further admonished man: **"Get not your friends by bare compliments, but by giving them sensible tokens of your love"**. We must come to the divine platform of living in Love, not in fear,

ANNOTATION:
Yes, earthman, work hard in silence and let your success be your noise.
Humble yourself in the journey of life and count others better than you are.

for the Peace and Justice of all humans.

A wise woman, Lao Russell, declared: **"Love is like unto the ascent of a high mountain peak. It comes ever nearer to you as you go ever nearer to it".** Love does not preach Peace outwardly and harbours wickedness in the inward parts of being. This is our problem. We must fight this manipulation by possessing the heart of Love in Peace and Justice.

The ancient King David prayed to God to salvage him from this manipulation, when he said: **"Draw me not away with the wicked, and with the workers of iniquity, which speak peace to their neighbours, but mischief is in their hearts"** (Psalms 28:3; KJV). He also admonished us to: **"Depart from evil, and do good; seek peace, and pursue it"** (Psalms 34:14;).

Oppression and injustice are expressions of lack of Love. These expressions also truncate peaceful co-existence amongst humans. In the Islamic

ANNOTATION:
We must do away with all forms of manipulation against love and peaceful co-existence. Let us walk on this path, individually and collectively.

book entitled '365 Sayings of Prophet Mohammed (Peace be upon him)', compiled and translated by AbdurRaheemKidwai, (pages 55 and 57), we read:

> *"Those dispensing justice fairly would be seated on the pulpits of light, to the right of God. They would be lavishly rewarded for having acted with justice even in cases involving their family and kith and kin ....Do not incur a victims curse upon you. For his supplication reaches God directly. God does not approve that anyone be oppressed".*

Oppression breeds lack of peaceful co-existence of humans; injustice is a catalyst to insecurity. We need Peace and we can find this in God-consciousness. God Himself is Peace, as well as **"the Giver of Peace",** as recorded in the

Koran. In the consciousness of peaceful co-existence of humans, we must stop hating and fighting ourselves due to our religious, tribal, cultural, racial and traditional differences, amongst other mundane factors.

THE BROTHERHOOD OF MAN

In the Shariyat, one of the ancient sacred writings of the Vairagi Lamas of Tibet, the earthman is admonished to rise, in symbolic terms, and touch the robe of God. This has to do with God-consciousness, spiritual mindedness and enlightenment. In this, peaceful co-existence is established. To this end, the Shariyat admonished:

"To the man who has touched the robe of God there is no distinction of race or belief, no consciousness of nationality, and no religious difference".

For the purpose of Peace and peaceful co-existence, especially in our nation and the entire world of man, we have to begin to see ourselves beyond the material camouflage of religions, tribes, regions, political associations, amongst other divisive tendencies. We must understand that beyond these camouflage systems, we are Souls and we are one in God, regardless of apparent divisions. We must strive to sincerely work for the Peace, Unity, Love, Oneness and Progress of all.

We must see ourselves in the light of the One Eternal Spirit of God that runs through all that is. This One Eternal Spirit is described as 'a golden thread' by a mastermind we know as Ralph Waldo. In his treatise on 'In Tune With The Infinite', this American great sage said:

"There is a golden thread that runs through every religion in the world. There is a golden

ANNOTATION:
God spoke in the 'Divine Iliad' thus: "Know thou then that 'I' alone lives; 'I' do not die, but out of Me comes both seeming life and death. Know thou also that the divisions of My thinking are but equal halves of One; for 'I' again say that I AM ONE; and all that comes from Me are One, but divided to appear as two".

thread that runs through the lives and teachings of all the prophets, seers, sages, and saviors in the world's history".

This is not the time for anyone to fold his hands in slothfulness for the agents of darkness to have dominion in our world. We have to be very serious and sincerely committed towards their transformation, by constantly sending them thoughts of Love and Peace daily. This is what we are expected to do. You have a role here; I have a role here too. This is the surest divine path of escape from the multitudinous vermin arising from the human agents of darkness in the world of man.

The ancient African wise men said that '**In a community where all the barbers have become cats, the rats must stop having their hair cut**'. Also, in their proverbial sayings, they made it known that '**When the bush is set on fire the chameleon will learn to walk fast**'. They

ANNOTATION:
It is said that justice and injustice are like day and night; they cannot stay together.
Earthman, you do not become taller by reducing other people's heights.

admonished that **'Whosoever that is prepared for lightning will not be taken unawares by thunder'**. They also did say that: **'It is better to flee danger and be laughed at than to face danger and be mourned later'**.

If we must give Peace of mind to others, we must first possess Peace of mind; for you can't give what you don't have. And to possess Peace, we must subjugate the quest for mundane aggrandizement. The great Chinese sage, Laotze, in his ancient treatise on 'The Simple Way' said, amongst other things, that: **"Not seeking the things of sense keeps the mind in peace"**. In one of the ancient sacred writings of Tibet, the earthman is admonished thus:

"The peace of society dependeth on justice; the happiness of individuals on the safe enjoyment of all their possessions.

"Keep the desires of thy heart, therefore, within the bounds of moderation; let the hand of justice lead them aright .

"In thy dealings with men, be impartial and just, do unto them as thou wouldst they should do unto thee.

"It is thy duty to be a friend to mankind, as it is thy interest that they should be friendly to thee".

God bless the reader.

ANNOTATION:
"It is thy duty to be a friend to mankind, as it is thy interest that they should be friendly to thee". A word is enough for the wise.

GOOD BEHAVIOUR CLEARS THE WAY FOR THE WELL-BEHAVED.

- The Harbinger

ANNOTATION:

Injustice and partiality are part of the rules in the mode of darkness.

WORK TOWARDS SOLUTION

Dear children of men in the world of man, for ages we have fought, maimed and killed ourselves for the sake of 'nothing'. What have we benefited from all these? What lessons have we

ANNOTATION:
Truly, we must be saved from ourselves. We must be saved from
lust, anger, greed, vanity and attachment to mundane things.

learnt? What truly is our gain from the path of violence? Are we humans incapable of living in Peace? If we truly desire to live in Love and Peace, we can live in Love and Peace, because God has made us capable of this.

However, let no government of the Earth-world arrogate to itself the sole authority to usher in lasting Peace and Justice in the world of man. And let no one think that the government will do it alone. Again, let no human institution of the Earth- world think that it can arbitrarily enforce peaceful co-existence on humans.

We must be prepared to live in Peace from our hearts. We must be prepared to learn from the past mistakes of our forefathers. Socrates said: **"Smart people learn from everything and everyone, average people from their experiences, stupid people already have all the answers"**. What the world needs now is the solution to the current dehumanised state of humanity, not just claiming to have solution without solution, but by contributing to the divine principles of solution individually and collectively.

I plead with all the governments and institutions of the earthmen: Let them encourage humans, using the powerful media networks at their disposal, and other organs, which includes but not limited to the United Nations, to encourage people to follow the divine path of solution. Let governments and institutions encourage the earthmen to send daily thoughts of Love and Peace to the vicious minded children of men in our world.

This may seem so insignificant, but the divine energy arising from this will certainly work for the benefit of all towards Love, Peace and Justice; towards peaceful co-existence of humans, to a far greater extent. This is a path that we haven't collectively followed as humans in the world of man.

ANNOTATION:
For ages, we haven't encouraged ourselves to follow the path of sending our energy daily, via mass and collective prayers, for the good of our world.

When we put collective efforts towards this path, even more than the manner that we put efforts in other things, we will change our world for good. Our efforts towards political campaigns, parliamentary activities, defence programmes, academic pursuits, individual businesses, amongst others, if we raise our efforts towards daily thoughts of Love in the consciousness of Peace, above them, in the course of time wickedness will be behind us.

Now, let us endeavour to send forth daily thoughts of Love, Peace and Justice to fellow earthmen and into the eco-systems of the Earth-world, whether or not we are encouraged to do so by governments and institutions of men. If this is done with sincere commitment, in no distant time, wickedness will diminish in our world. This is one of the best and easiest ways to transform the misguided world to Love, Peace and Justice.

ANNOTATION:
The ear does not need to be as broad as a mat in order to hear well. It is said that an army of sheep led by a lion will defeat an army of lions led by a goat.

HEAVEN IS WAITING FOR EARTHMEN

The God of Heaven is patiently waiting for the earthman to come to Him and be saved from himself. And until man does this, the agony arising from his delay, is his own making. And this delay is caused by our ignorance and wrong thinking, which feeds certain realms of darkness that must be fed to ruin us.

The thoughts of hate, wickedness, rape, arson, terrorism, kidnapping, assassination, corruption, robbery, amongst other hideous thoughts, are amongst our major problems. They are nothing but the outcome of ignorance and wrong thinking – the mode of darkness – as far as the nature of divine reality is concerned. These thoughts constitute the basis of awaiting, and in them lies our agony. The earthmen are told that God Himself spoke in the Divine Iliad thus:

ANNOTATION:
The ignorance of man regarding the nature of reality -- the true essence of existence -- is the bane of his peace and true progress of life.

"I am a patience God. All men will come to Me in due time, but the agony of awaiting that day shall be theirs alone.

"And that day shall not come until man himself shall cleanse himself from his own unbalanced thinking".

The time has come for all men to learn and live by the sacred laws of the brotherhood of all existences, encapsulated in Love, Peace and Justice in mercy. Those of you, earthmen, versed in diverse sacred writings, are aware that this was part of the message which an Extraterrestrial Intelligence – Cherubim Ramasa– gave to the earthman we know as Levi.

Levi H. Dowling was brought forth in the Spirit into the realm of the 24 Ancient Ones, the 24 Elders or Cherubims and Seraphims,

ANNOTATION:
The Holy Bible says that 'there is time for everything'. The time wherein we live now, is the time of the Light of God for the world of man. And whether man likes it or not, love and peace must rule at last.

guardians of the 'Circle of the Central Sun'. The transfer of power and dominion from the guardians of the previous age to the guardians of the present age was revealed to him in the Heavenly realms of Light. When he wanted to write certain things that he heard, as recorded in the introduction of 'The Aquarian Gospel', Cherubim Ramasa admonished him thus:

> ***"Not now, my son, not now; but you may write it down for men when men have learned the sacred laws of Brotherhood, of Peace on Earth, good- will to every living thing".***

Now, the time has come. Remember one of the immortal blessings pronounced on the earthmen by the Great Lord Jesus the Christ; it goes thus: **"Blessed are the peacemakers: for they shall be called the children of God"** (Math. 5:9; KJV).

ANNOTATION:
"Blessed are the peacemakers: for they shall be called the children of God". Peace brings us into the most elevated, auspicious and benevolent recognition of divine sonship in the holy strata of the Almighty God.

This pronouncement by the Lord Himself shows the eternal validity of Peace in the divine spheres. It shows that the prime evidence of divine existence is not premised on religious denomination, but upon the practical demonstration of Peace in Love.

This entails, amongst other things, the maintenance of Peace within a person, within the family unit, amongst neighbours, in the community, in a nation and the world at large. Peace and Justice in Love, the sacred principles of brotherhood of all existences, must begin within you, radiate in the family, and from there spread outward. Without Peace in Love, even a family is ruined. In the ancient Niti Sastra, Canakya Pandita, one of the wisest men of the East, said:

> ***"The goddess of fortune personally comes to that place where fools are not worshipped, where grains***

ANNOTATION:
Failure to maintain peace and love in a home, is a catalyst of the manipulations and dominion of the forces of darkness in that home.

are carefully stocked, and where there are no quarrels between husband and wifew

"It is better to have one son with good qualities than to have one hundred foolish sons.

"Innumerable stars cannot dissipate the darkness,but one moon can illuminate the darkness of night".

GREETINGS OF PEACE

The higher divine spheres of being are fully aware that without Love, Peace and Justice in mercy, in the world of man, all efforts of true progress and divine ascent will be thwarted. Thus, some denizens of the divine spheres are engaged, from time to time, in the art of salvaging the earthman from himself– from his vicious mind, from ignorance and wrong thinking.

ANNOTATION:
The mighty Forces of Light above do not see us the way we see ourselves. They see us as one family of humanity, but we see ourselves as black, white, rich, poor, and from the reference point of our religions, amongst others.

When we see the entire children of men as our neighbours, and endeavour at all times to give Peace to our neighbours, we will greatly diminish wickedness and insecurity. I am confident that the importance of Peace in the world of man usually prompts the Lord Himself, great Angelic Beings from above and some enlightened minds to often send us the greetings of Peace.

Remember what Jethro, the father-in-law of the great Prophet Moses, said to him when he was about sending him forth: **"And Jethro said to Moses, go in peace"** (Exo. 4:18; KJV). What was the manner of greetings of the great Angelic One from above to Prophet Daniel? He said thus to the Prophet: **"Peace be unto thee"** (Dan. 10:19; KJV).

Also, the Great Lord Jesus the Christ admonished: **"And into whatsoever house ye**

ANNOTATION:
Peace is so important that, without it, man cannot excel in Light in the journey of life.

enter, first say, Peace be to this house" (Luke 10:5; KJV). Again, based on the divine messages he received, the Prophet Mohammed (Peace be upon him) proclaimed the greetings of Peace in the world of man, as well as peaceful co-existence of humans. Even today, true Muslims know that those killing and maiming innocent humans, in the pretence of fighting for God, are discrediting the true essence of Islam.

In the Hadith, translated by AbdurRaheemKidwai, the Prophet Mohammed (Peace be upon him) said: **"The archangel Gabriel (who brought divine revelation to me) impressed upon me so much the command for treating neighbours well that I thought neighbours would get a share also in inheritance"**. It is also reported in the Hadith thus:

*"The Prophet (peace be upon him) was informed about a woman who was **known***

ANNOTATION:
The terrorists, some of which are Islamic extremists,
kill fellow earthmen in the guise of fighting for the Almighty.
They know not that they are merely feeding the hosts of darkness.

for her devotion to prayer, fasting and charity. However, she used to hurt her neighbours with her offensive comments. He dubbed her as an inmate of Hell. On the contrary, he branded another woman as a dweller of Paradise who was kind to her neighbours, though she did not perform any extra Prayer".

MAINTAIN PEACE ALWAYS

Distinguished ladies and gentlemen of the world of man, when we talk about 'Peace and Security', it is by maintaining Peace and Justice in Love in our neighbourhood, that we can maintain Peace in our nations and our world. Today, we are faced with diverse security challenges. We are aware that there are agents of darkness in our midst. By the quest to acquire money, property, women, land, amongst other mundane things, they shed human blood.

ANNOTATION:
Man's mundane attempt to dominate his fellow man, offers nothing to the world of man than the flow of blood. And as blood calls before the Throne, the hunter will be the hunted.

Through multifarious channels, which includes but not limited to kidnapping, cultism, terrorism, armed robbery, corruption, arson, subtle cum outright rebellion, the dirty job of assassination and hypocrisy, they waste the blood of fellow earthmen. I have always maintained that we cannot defeat these hideous ones only by the force of arms.

We must all be concerned and, as earlier stated, send them constant thoughts of Love for their transformation. Let us not pass over this lightly, because in divine terms, the platform upon which I stand, this is amongst the foremost ways forward in our search for national and global Peace.

We must learn from the prayers offered to the Lord by Prahlada Maharaja, wise King of ancient India. This prayer, recorded in the 7th volume, chapter 9 verse 43 of Srimad-

ANNOTATION:
The dominion of darkness is about to end in the world of man.
Sanity will reign in the years ahead, but you have a part to play
now in the framework of divine Light.

Bhagavatam, one of the Vedic sacred writings, teaches the earthman to be focused on the Lord and to send thoughts of Love to the materialistic sons and daughters of men. It also shows that the undue quest for mundane things, in the guise of religion, politics, tradition or whatever, is not the path of the wise. The prayer goes thus:

"O best of the great personalities, I am not at all afraid of material existence, for wherever I stay I am fully absorbed in thoughts of Your glories and activities.

"My concern is only for the fools and rascals who are making elaborate plans for material happiness and maintaining their families, societies and countries.

ANNOTATION:

All those who are situated on the mode of goodness in the journey of life, must be seriously concerned about the misguided earthmen situated in the mode of darkness and troubling our world. We must pray for them always.

I am simply concerned with love for them".

In our world today, some earthmen are engaged in the destruction of property, killing and maiming fellow earthmen, in the guise of fighting for the Almighty God, whilst claiming to be believers. They kill innocent citizens and persons who have done them no wrong, thereby contributing to insecurity on the physical realms of Earth. In the Koran, it is made absolutely clear that such persons have no portion in the Light of the Almighty God. Consequently, the Koran warned thus:

> ***"There are some who declare: 'We believe in Allah and the Last Day', yet they are not believers.***
>
> ***"They seek to deceive Allah, and those who believe in Him: but they deceive none save themselves, though***

ANNOTATION:
Those who "seek to deceive Allah", by terrorising and murdering fellow earthmen in the name of God, are situated in the lowest systems of the mode of darkness".

they may not perceive it. There is a sickness in their hearts which Allah has increased: they shall be sternly punished because they lie.

"When it is said to them: 'Do not commit evil in the land', they reply: 'We do nothing but good'. But it is they who are the evil-doers, though they may not perceive it" (Koran 2:8—12).

God bless the reader.

THRESHOLD OF WINNOWING

Dear people of Planet Earth, whether or not we know it, whether the governments of the Earth-world know it or not, the Earth- world today stands upon the threshold of Planetary winnowing.

This is well known and made clear by Extraterrestrial Intelligences of Light in the Heavenly realms. I spoke extensively on this subject in my book entitled **'Deeper Realities of Existence Vol. 1'**.

On this platform of Planetary winnowing, the era in which we live, speaking in relative terms, our Planet may rise or fall. The dangers of atomic radiation, terrorism, viruses, amongst other destructive elements and vicious mundane mind-sets and activities, all seek to pull down the Earth-world and the children of men.

It is only the Divine Potency of Love, radiated in our hearts by the Holy Spirit, that can salvage the earthmen. This will bring about Peace and Justice, required for the rise of the earthmen into the Light of the Kingdom of God, wherein Peace abides on Earth. This is the hour for all to be involved, to salvage our world from the core agents of darkness. Consequently, the best and easiest way to bring forth Peace on Earth, is for all to strive to possess Peace and constantly radiate same from the deepest centres of our hearts and minds.

ANNOTATION:
Great battle is being waged now by the Forces of Light, under the divine authority of the King of Kings and Lord of Lords, to banish all that stand against the divine rise of Earth in Light.

DON'T PROCRASTINATE

Don't wait for any person to give you Peace, rather possess Peace within yourself to give Peace to others. Don't wait for the government to give you Peace, because if you are a child of Peace, you will give Peace even to the government and people of the Earth-world.

Sevenfold blessed is the one who lives in a state of inner Peace, whose actions disturb no one, and who is not disturbed by the actions of anyone. This state of consciousness is required now; it is required from each and everyone of us. You must live in Peace within to give Peace out at all times.

We must imbibe true knowledge cum practical application of divine Love, in order for us to maintain Peace and Justice, to live in Peace. First of all, the knowledge of Peace is very important in this connection. In the Bhagavad-Gita, earlier quoted in this material, given to the earthmen about 5000 years ago, we are told that God said to humans:

ANNOTATION:
Blessed is the one who disturbs no one, and who is disturbed by no one. This state of consciousness is achieved within the ambit of the Universal Law of Balance, by which the mind is embedded in the true divine state of ballance and troubled of nothing -- the state of mastermind.

"Verily there is no purifier in this world like knowledge. The man who is full of faith, who is devoted to it, and who has subdued all the senses, obtains this knowledge; and, having obtained the knowledge, he goes at once to the supreme peace". (Bhag-G. 4: 38,39).

"There is no knowledge of the Self to the unsteady, and to the unsteady no meditation is possible; and to the un- meditative there can be no peace He attains peace into whom all desires enter as waters enter the ocean, which, filled from all sides, remains unmoved; but not the man full of desires".(Bhag-G. 2:66,70).

TIME FOR ACTION

Dear reader of this material, in all the Holy Scriptures and in all the sacred writings worldwide, God has spoken more than enough for Peace and peaceful co-existence. Extraterrestrial Intelligences and the masterminds of all ages have spoken extensively on Love, Peace and Justice in mercy.

The earthmen have been given more than enough information on the practical art of peaceful co-existence of humans and oneness with the Almighty God. We have been given enough information about peaceful co-existence. Whoever fails in this connection does so not because divine guidance wasn't provided, but because he hasn't practically put into practice the divine guidance from above.

The expected end of man by God is Peace, but we must diligently seek God, the Lord of Peace, to live within the framework of Peace in our world. And the time to act is now. God and the

ANNOTATION:
Earthman, expand your consciousness, your perception and values of existence, in the mode of goodness of your Creator. Your efforts therein will never be in vain

Mighty Forces of Heavenly Light seek always to guide us on the path of Love,

Peace and Justice in mercy. Whosoever seeks this path will be so guided. In the Holy Bible, God Himself said:

> *"For I know the thoughts that I think toward you, saith the LORD, thoughts of peace, and not of evil, to give you an expected end.*
>
> *Then shall ye call upon Me, and ye shall go and pray unto Me, and I will hearken unto you. And ye shall seek Me, and find Me, when ye shall search for Me with all your heart".*
> *(Jer. 29:11-13; KJV).*

God bless the reader.

ANNOTATION:
The earthman is blessed and lifted in the journey of life by fully submitting his mind and senses to the Words of the One Eternal Almighty God. His Words are embedded into the realities of love, peace and justice in mercy for all creatures, including the children of men.

BEYOND THE MUNDANE

In the Gospel as recorded by Saint John, the Great Lord Jesus the Christ said: **"Peace I leave with you, My peace I give unto you: not as the world giveth, give I unto you. Let not your heart be troubled, neither let it be**

ANNOTATION:
Christ didn't say 'houses, wives, husbands, chariots or clothes I leave with you'. Rather, He said 'Peace I leave with you'. Don't forget that.

afraid" heart be troubled, neither let it be afraid" (Jn.14:27; KJV). Here, we note a dichotomy as related to Peace, namely, the Peace of the Lord and the peace of the world.

For ages, the earthmen, via diverse mundane institutions, have strived for peace in mundane terms. This hasn't worked out because of the frailties of the children of men in our lower mundane aspects of being. Apart from our lower aspects in this material world, we humans also have our essential higher aspects of reality. Peace enacted from our mundane aspects, is referred to by the Lord as the 'peace of the world'.

The peace of the world comes in a manner which may not give inner Peace to all the parties involved. When the United Nations sends out a 'peace keeping force' to a warring enclave on Earth, for instance, relative 'peace' may be restored to that area via the armed forces empowered by the United Nations to do so. That is the peace of the world.

ANNOTATION:
Without the Holy Spirit, peace will elude us. He who tries to shake a tree stump shakes only himself.

We must learn how to enact Peace on Earth from our essential higher aspects, beyond the elements of the so-called 'peace' generated from our mundane aspects. The higher aspects of Peace flows from the divine spheres into the hearts and minds of men, via the 'Higher Self'. It is encapsulated in Love whilst its operational code is 'Justice and Mercy' for all.

MAN'S MUNDANE LIMITATIONS

As humans, we must understand that we are set forth by God to know ourselves. It is your right to know yourself, but whether or not you do so is the making of your volition. You should know that you are an identity far beyond the camouflage systems of the physical realms of Earth. You should know that your consciousness is not limited to the physical aspects of life generally known.

ANNOTATION:
It is said: 'Man, know thyself'. This is very important for each Soul personality in the human embodiment.

You should know that both identity and consciousness precede your physical reality; and that part of your mission here and now includes but not limited to contributing to the sanity of existence. Each Soul personality should endeavour not to fail in this mission. And our success in this mission lies in upholding Love, Peace and Justice in mercy.

However, our failures come when we become solely attached to the limitations, defects and frailties of the gross material body. And on this platform we can't absorb nor generate genuine Peace for all humans. The ancient Sanskrit 'acaryas' revealed in the Upanishads that the actions of the earthman, within the limitations of his lower aspects, are governed by four major defects, namely:

(i)   Man is sure to commit mistakes,

(ii)   Man is invariably illusioned,

(iii)   Man is limited by imperfect senses, and

(iv)   Man has the tendency to cheat others.

With these frailties and limitations, the earthman cannot generate and manifest the needed Peace, because his earth- life is embedded with the framework of his lower self. He must rise above the limited propensities of his lower aspects, and come into the divine propensities of his higher nature, for the needed Peace to flow.

Peace, emanating from the Holy Spirit, can only be absorbed and radiated by the earthman from the dimension of his higher essential aspects. It is only from man's 'Higher Self' that Peace, defined as 'freedom from disturbance' or 'quiet and tranquillity', can be experienced and expressed. And anyone who doesn't contribute to Love, Peace and Justice; who contributes nothing to the peaceful co-existence of all humans in mercy for all, is merely existing, but not 'alive', in the Creation of the Almighty God.

ANNOTATION:
Are you alive in the Light of the Creation of the Almighty or are you merely existing?

THE WELLBEING OF ALL

When you have Peace and express same in Love, even in man's scientific terms, you are the first beneficiary, as the originating point. This is also in accordance with the inexorable Universal Laws. To this end, thoughts of balanced Justice in Love with Peace of mind, activate the release of benevolent brain chemicals, including endorphins, within the ambit of good feelings for individual's wellbeing and sound health. The thoughts of hate and wickedness, on the other hand, activate the release of stress hormones, which are disadvantageous to man's wellbeing.

Therefore, the needed Peace now is the Peace flowing from the 'Centre of the Heart of Hearts' – God – to the hearts of the sons and daughters of men. These are the hearts which have imbibed the true Love of God. This Peace is embedded with total forgiveness to all offenders. Without forgiveness and Love, the Spirit of Peace and Justice will not come forth in the life of a person.

ANNOTATION:
The pure in heart is the embodiment of love and peace.
Grudges, great impediment in man's divine relationship with
Heaven, is absent in a pure heart.

And anyone who doesn't have Peace cannot radiate same to others.

Therein lies the difference between the Peace of God and the peace of the world. We are very much aware of how we, the children of men, go about the maintenance of peace in our world. The governments of our world use the police, the military, imprisonment, amongst other things, to maintain so- called peace. Evidently, this hasn't achieved the needed result, based on the evidence of security challenges facing our world today.

Nevertheless, we must sincerely appreciate the efforts of the government of different nations, including our country Nigeria, towards peace. We must be appreciative, especially to the security men and women who lay down their lives to physically secure the lives of citizens. However, we must understand that this alone will not usher in the needed Peace in our nation and

ANNOTATION:
If the government of the nations of the Earth-world could usher in lasting peace on Earth, this would have been achieved. The Holy Spirit alone is the giver of peace.

in all the nations of the Earth-world. We must come to the path of divine enlightenment for the needed Peace and Justice to flow.

Pope Francis, during the celebration of the 2020 'World Peace Day', instituted by Pope Paul VI, mentioned that **"Peace is a path of hope, a path on which one advances through dialogue, reconciliation and conversion"**. For true reconciliation to be achieved in our hearts, we must learn to forgive all offenders, regardless of their offences.

FORGIVENESS AS PREREQUISITE FOR PEACE

Forgiveness and Love are the fundamental basis for Peace and Justice, individually and collectively. This is the verdict of God in His diverse manifestations, Extraterrestrial Intelligences of Light, as well as all the divinely inspired masterminds, past and present. Without total forgiveness for all offenders, Peace will elude the earthmen.

ANNOTATION:
Mundane enlightenment is different from divine enlightenment.
On the platform of divine enlightenment, Intelligences above the earthman are properly situated to provide guidance.

Forgiveness, in absolute divine terms, is the prime basis for Love. Peace and Justice separate the consciousness of the earthman from that of the beasts. Mercy is the nectar of benevolent reciprocal action from the divine dimension. This is the core message of the Spirit of God in Light. In our time also, this is the message of **'The Sole Spiritual Head'**, whose divine authority and existence lies even far beyond the divine domain of the 'Supreme Lords of Creation'.

I am speaking here about the personality known as **'Great Leader Olumba Olumba Obu'**, whose words in our time are recorded in the holy book we know as **'The Everlasting Gospel'**. He has once again brought Love in the message of Peace and Justice, with mercy for all, to our world; as well as the greetings of Peace to the children of men. He is practically demonstrating these in our time, as a guide to the earthmen. He declared in **'The Everlasting Gospel'** (TEG) thus:

ANNOTATION:
Forgiveness and mercy, as taught and practically demonstrated by
Great Leader Olumba Olumba Obu in our time,
is certainly worthy of emulation.

"*If someone calls you a thief or murderer, abuses you, steals from you, kills your relation or a member of your family, do not count sin on him.*

"*You must forgive and forget. If someone commits adultery with your wife, assassinates your character and that of your wife, or worse still unlawfully impregnates your daughter, burns down your home or destroys your property will-fully or not, you are duty-bound to forgive and forget.*

"*If someone lies against you, or in fact deals with you nonchalantly,*

ANNOTATION:
To forgive and forget is on the divine platform of reality; this is difficult for the earthmen in the mode of darkness.

commits any act or manner of sin or atrocity against you, it is your responsibility to forgive him and forget what he has done against you.

"This Gospel is founded on Truth. It is salvation to those who believe and practice it, but damnation to those who ignore it "(TEG.Vol. 1, 23:8—12).

"The children of peace do not fight against any person, for they remain in peace with everyone.

"They are those who will inherit the Kingdom of God.

ANNOTATION:
Forgiveness is Love and Light flowing from the divine spheres of the Holy Spirit.

"If from the beginning of the world, peace had been in the world, what need could the armed forces serve". (TEG. Vol. 2, 13:14,15).

"The real children of God do not quarrel, fight, lie, hate, or engage in any form of violence.

"The children of God do not identify themselves with anything violent. Even when a child of God is abused, he has to return peace If you fail to be peaceful in your everyday life, you are killing yourself gradually.

"Peace is indispensable for your existence". (TEG. Vol. 3, 79:10,11,22).

Furthermore, **'His Holiness Olumba Olumba Obu'**, though misunderstood by some earthmen of our time, via malicious and misguided campaigns of calumny, has nonetheless brought the practical basis of Love, Peace and Justice in mercy to the world of man. He has brought practical basis of peaceful co-existence of all humans, in the consciousness of the brotherhood of all existences, to the world of man in a big way, in this generation of men.

He has consistently pronounced and practically demonstrated Love, Peace and Justice, as the core basis of truly advanced spiritual civilisation, for all generations of the children of men. He doesn't take any physical action against all offenders, in any manner. This is well known to divinely enlightened minds. Because of this, certain bogus earthmen take advantage of it to continue on the path of falsehood in their campaigns of calumny. Thus, **'His Holiness Olumba Olumba Obu'** is a practical example to the earthmen on how to uphold Love,

ANNOTATION:
For long, the earthman has advanced in all sorts of mundane things. Our so-called civilization is purely mundane. Spiritual civilization will finally dominate the world of man and dwarf the consciousness of materialism.

Peace and Justice in mercy for all, in the world of man.

His declarations of Peace between man and his fellow men, between man and the elements of creation, between man and Spirits in the Universe, between man and the entire creation, between man and the Almighty God, are well known. He admonished the earthmen, regarding the challenges we face today, **"To embrace The Holy Spirit and live by His guidance",** and also said:

*"**Divisions, war, democracy, and** sophisticated weapons of mass destruction are not the solution to the ever-increasing problem of mankind. All that is needed to solve the problems of Nigeria, and the world at large, is the practice of love and more love. Let your thoughts, words and **actions be***

guided by the overwhelming desire to love and live in brotherhood" *(New Kingdom Trumpet; Vol. 21 No. 5, May 2021, p.9 & 28).*

God bless the reader.

ANNOTATION:
'Brotherhood' in this connection is spoken of in the light of the oneness of God and His Creation. This oneness is only enacted by love, not otherwise.

IF YOU VALUE YOUR HEAD DON'T ALLOW DAGGER NEAR YOUR THROAT.

- The Harbinger

ANNOTATION:

He who holds another down also holds down himself.

EARTH IN THE THRESHOLD OF WINNOWING

My lovely people of the world of man, as earlier stated, the Earth-world now stands upon the threshold of Planetary winnowing. The earthman has gradually come into the generation and the hour of regeneration, in which all things on Earth will have a new beginning. Whether or not this is known, the Lord of the Universe – True Owner of Earth – will surely establish Peace and Justice on the physical realms of Earth, with a Mighty Spiritual Power never before known to the children of men. This was amongst other things revealed to Saint John in 96 AD thus:

> *"And the seventh angel sounded; and there were great voices in heaven, saying, The kingdoms of this world are become the kingdoms of our Lord, and of his Christ; and he shall reign for ever and ever .*

> *"And the nations were angry, and thy wrath is come, and the time of the dead, that they should be judged, and that thou shouldest give reward unto thy servants the*

ANNOTATION:
"The kingdoms of this world are become the kingdoms of our Lord, and of His Christ". This is about to play out on Earth in a big way.

prophets, and to the saints, and them that fear thy name, small and great; and shouldest destroy them which destroy the earth" (Rev. 11:15,18; KJV).

All the destroyers of men – destroyers of Planet Earth – should be warned: This era is the long foretold era of the end-time: Let the destroyers of men stop behaving like 'a fowl that is drunk', because the 'drunken fowl' is about to meet with a 'mad wolf' lurking in the corner. In the entire history of the earthmen, this is the most dangerous hour for anyone to uphold the life of wickedness and evil practices. The peace of this world, and the divine progress thereof, are firmly in the Hands of The Owner of the Universe. This is no joke.

One Extraterrestrial Intelligence told the **Harbinger of the Last Covenant** that **"The Seal of the King of Kings and Lord of Lords has**

ANNOTATION:
Whoever wants to continue on the path of wickedness in the world of man will have himself to blame in this hour of fulfilment.

now completed judgement on Earth; what is going on now is the execution of His divine judgement". And remember that the King of Kings and Lord of Lords was called **"Faithful and True",** and it was said that **"in righteousness He doth judge and make war".** (See Rev. 19:11--21).

Also, remember the parable of the 'prodigal son' given to the earthmen by the Lord Jesus the Christ. When the prodigal son returned to his father at last, his father said amongst other things: **"For this my son was dead, and is alive again".**(See Luke 15:11--25). This individual – the prodigal son – wasn't physically dead, but it was said to him that '**he was dead and alive again'.** When was he 'dead?' It was when he separated himself from his father. His 'father' here was mentioned by the Lord in symbolic terms, representing the Light of God.

All the earthmen who are in the mode of darkness, are separated from the Divine Light

The One called Faithfull and True -- King of Kings and Lord of Lords -- now leads the hosts of the Forces of Light in the final battle to reclaim our world for the Light of His Kingdom.

of the One Eternal Almighty God. And in the light of the divine essence of reality in the Holy Spirit, they are spiritually 'dead'. The mental stances and projections of these 'dead' earthmen empower the deadly forces of darkness frolicking in our world with diverse destructive elements. But now, the hour has come, and it was said (where we earlier read in Revelation 11) thus: **"and thy wrath is come, and the time of the dead, that they should be judged".**

Now, the phrase, **"thy wrath is come",** referring to the Lord of Creation, has nothing to do with wrath, exasperation or anger as known to the children of men. It was used as a metaphor to represent the human interpretation of what will happen here on Earth, which the earthmen will see, in our human terms, as occurring via the 'anger' of God.

Let it be known that great calamities and upheavals are on the way to the physical realms of Earth,

ANNOTATION:
The "dead men" who empower the vicious astral forces against the world of man should either resurrect from the "grave" now or be permanently vanquished.

which the "dead men" of the Earth-world won't survive. And in this connection, the COVID-19 Pandemic is a mere 'warning shot' in divine terms. The war of wars is on the way, but no human gun or bomb will be used. All those situated in the mode of goodness, as well as the higher mode of divine nature, especially the earthmen spiritually designated now as 'chosen ones', will be salvaged. This will occur in a manner that is presently beyond human comprehension.

The mighty Forces of Light above, under the authority of the **King of Kings and Lord of Lords,** have stored enough energy of divine Light, in possessing the 'right' to bring this to pass. They are so committed to this – to salvage the Earth in the Light of Heaven – that they don't mind if the end result requires that the earthmen will begin a new life even in the desert, as the worst possible scenario.

ANNOTATION:
The COVID-19 Pandemic is a mere warning shot to the Earth-world; greater calamities are on the way, which the earthmen have built up for ages against themselves.

The forces of darkness are also so committed to the project of the impending war of wars, to the extent that they don't mind at all even if the Earth Planet is completely destroyed in the process. However, the energies of divine Light will come forth so strong against the multifarious chambers of darkness, to dismantle the vicious energies of darkness, the 'right' thereof, causing such energies to revert in mutilation and return to their starting points.

Now, the aforementioned 'starting points' in this connection are the sons and daughters of men in the mode of darkness, including some who are embedded in the mode of passion. They are the primordial origins of the vicious energies of darkness in the first place, by which the forces of darkness appropriate and possess the 'right' to exercise dominion in the world of man. What I am saying now have diverse mysteries not explained. However, the coming war of wars will heavily weigh more on the

ANNOTATION:
If you are identified as a starting point for the radiation of the vicious energy of darkness, then put yourself in serious prayer now, because of what is about to play out.

human channels of darkness, in consideration of all generations, regardless of whether one appears religious at the moment or not.

ENTHRONEMENT OF DIVINE LIGHT ON EARTH

Earthmen, be warned: Shortly, the people of this world will be bamboozled by what will be played out on Earth. The calamities that will come upon this world will completely dwarf the experiences of the earthmen in the days of old, as far as what we know as 'destruction' is concerned. With a Mighty Power never before experienced in the world of man, the Holy Spirit will tear down the ethereal layers of wickedness for the supreme enthronement of Love, Peace and Justice in the world of man.

Leaders and rulers of the nations of men, and all the earthmen, should have this in mind, as we continue in our limited mundane quest for sustainable peace and justice. Blessed is the one who will rise above this limited quest and come to the divine platform, by upholding and transmitting the daily consciousness of Love, Peace and Justice in mercy for all.

This is the era of Love, Peace and Divine Justice, whether or not we know it. All the efforts and prayers of the lovers of Peace, in all the past generations of men, even hitherto, are now supremely potentized into factors of several folds. The earthman is oblivious of this, rather he is like a man whose house is on fire, but instead of putting off the fire he is busy chasing after rats.

As I speak to you now, I am fully aware that there are great Extraterrestrial Intelligences, (Mighty Angelic Beings of Light), situated in the great mission to salvage the Earth in Light. They work strictly under the immutable Divine authority of the **One Eternal King of Kings and Lord of Lords**, who is set to bring forth the benevolent conditions under which the

ANNOTATION:
This is the era of love, the era of peace, the era of the mode of goodness; therefore, the earthman must comply to divine Light or give way.

Earth-world will flourish in the Light of Heaven.

Some of these Intelligences (Forces of Light) spoken of, are the riders of the 'Star No. 3', situated at 1,555 miles above the surface of Earth in a shield of invisibility. They come four times every year in our time, in an operation of many years to come. **Mission**: Potentization of each thought, word or action of Love – selfless divine service to God and man – into a factor of 3,000; stored in the hidden parliament of the Forces of Light. **Usage**: To dwarf the forces of darkness in the war of wars to come. **Authority**: The King of Kings and Lord of Lords.

Earthmen, the foregoing is not a matter that we should begin to argue about. I am not interested in that. The answer to any argument is what will happen shortly. It is said that experience is the best teacher. Just wait and see. But let me emphasize it once again that the final phase of the enthronement of Love, Peace and Justice on Earth will come about via a great battle never

ANNOTATION:
The high Angelic riders of 'Star No. 3', the holy ones from above, work for the overall benefit of the family of humanity, under the immutable authority of the King of Kings and Lord of Lords.

before experienced; a battle wherein the COVID-19 Pandemic will be a child's play; a non-physical battle bereft of human armaments, which even the combined forces of the earthly super powers can't comprehend nor withstand. It is the long foretold **'battle of the LORD of Hosts'** that will finally end all battles and wars on the physical realms of Earth. And let it be known, as earlier stated, that the COVID-19 Pandemic is a mere 'warning shot' for the 'impending doom' against the channels and instruments of darkness.

STAND OUT OF THE CROWD

Distinguished ladies and gentlemen of our Planet, our foremost duty now is to continue to uphold Love, Peace and Justice, by living in Love and Peace at all times. Love is the consummate Divine Energy that cannot ever be defeated, because of its potency to multiply itself by itself. In one of my books entitled **'Great Divine Impact'**, I expressed this thus:

ANNOTATION:
You have heard of the final battle of the "LORD of Hosts", as
recorded in the Holy Bible. You think it won't occur?
Just watch and see.

"Love is the only Universal Power that increases Itself by Itself. If you show forth Love and It is rejected, the potency of that Love will return back to you, be multiplied four times and go back to your initial target, until It prevails. Nothing can permanently block the potency of Love, absolutely nothing. It is the final and the consummate weapon of the saints".

Dear reader, this is the hour for all humans to work hard with the Holy Spirit, in the great divine mission of building ideal humans – real men – who will live in Love, Peace and Justice, with mercy for all. **'The Grail Message'** of Abd-ru- shin admonished us thus:

> ***"Now try to recognize the people who truly strive for the ideal here on Earth, and help them with their activity, because their building up will only bring benefit".***

It is also my desire that, we will be such persons working to build our families, communities, nations and our world in Love, Peace and Justice, with mercy for all; in our thoughts, words and actions. **Oh Almighty God, may we – the children of men – never depart from this noble path.**

Dear lovely earthmen, as I conclude this material, I urge you to make enough time to read it again and again. Endeavour to understand and act on these things. It is said that **'if you give a stammerer enough time he will pronounce his father's name'.** Be firm and committed to the message herein exposed. Stand out of the crowd on this matter, and stand alone in God.

ANNOTATION:
Be firm, be steadfast in the Light of God; pray for the good of all, and your reward from above is as sure as day light.

It is easier to stand with the crowd; it takes courage to stand alone.

As you stand alone in the Light of the Almighty God, you are surely not alone. But in the Light of God, work hard and reap the fruits of good labour. I say to you, in accordance with the Universal Law of Reciprocal Action, you are the first beneficiary of your labour in the mode of goodness. It is said that **'the mouth greased with palm-oil by feeding fat is brought about by hands soiled with hard-work'**.

You have heard that **'Heaven helps those who help themselves'**. The subject of this material is a serious issue for daily practical action. It is said by the wise ones of Africa that **'you can discuss a small matter while standing up; but for a big matter which lasts long, you have to settle down'**. Make those who are near you happy and those far will come. Any message sent to the sky by the rising smoke will surely get there.

ANNOTATION:
Heaven helps those who help themselves. This is not by going to seek 'help' from the realms of darkness, but by upholding the consciousness of love, peace and justice in mercy for all.

CONCLUSION

Earthmen, in conclusion, one thing is certain in this my open letter: life on Earth is full of hidden things; things generally unknown. The unknown is part of the mystery of life, and the unknown is part of you now. From the point of birth to the point of departure (death), the earthman is encapsulated by hidden things about himself. Even some of the subtle things that he should know about himself, he doesn't know them, primarily because of his intense mental and emotional focus on the physical things of the earth-life.

Earthman, the words you speak, which you know, hold some fabrics of the unknown aspects of your being. And in this terms, dear reader, the dumb speaks as well. The words you speak, therefore, are offshoots of your mental act in their initial proclivities. The words then count as 'words' in the mental matrix, whether you are dumb or not.

ANNOTATION:
Earthman, the 'unknown' is part of you now. The most important person in the world is 'you'. You are far more than what you know in the human terms.

The earthman may ask: 'What is the unknown in this?' When the earthman is taken into the mystery of words, he will have a clue about many unknown things. He may even have a better clue about the beginning and the end of his gross material body in the world of man; the experience that we know as 'death'. Earthman, know and understand that, from the moment you are born on Earth, some specific numbers of words are assigned to you to speak, after which you speak no more within the framework of your physical camouflage systems. Speaking no more in this terms, therefore, is death.

The number of words assigned to you to speak in the world of man, before your physical birth, are planted in the subtle systems of your psyche chromosomes. This planting is done in the realms we know as 'in-between-life'. This realm is neither where you are coming from nor where you are going to. Rather, it is the realm between both. The Soul personality coming to the physical realms of Earth, from diverse original home of Souls, must step down first into the

---

ANNOTATION:
When the earthman passes through the experience we know as 'death', he speaks no more on the physical realms of Earth.

realms of in- between-life before physical manifestation.

In the in-between-life, the personality to be born acquires destiny in the absolute and probable aspects, and assigned the number of words to speak in the world of man. (For more on the in-between-life, as well as the absolute and probable destiny, see my book entitled **'Hidden Truth of Man and Woman'**). The number of the assigned words, to this end, in the in-between-life, are configured and embedded in the universal pool of probabilities. This is in conjunction, however, with some aspects of the absolute dimension of destiny.

Furthermore, the number of words which you are granted to speak on the physical realms of Earth, deals only with the number and not with the words themselves. The number deals with the amount of words which the earthman will speak and speak no more. But the words to speak themselves are in the probable systems of reality.

ANNOTATION:
The book, Hidden Truth of Man and Woman', contains divine messages from above in our time, and is highly recommended for the people of our world.

Consequently, you can't speak beyond the number of words assigned to you, but you can choose the words to speak from the pool of thought-probabilities, by the volition of your mind, the rudiments thereof. This letter – **save us from ourselves** – has admonished us to choose our words from the comfort zone of divine Light and give life, not pain, to others. By so doing, you will be a major contributor to the sacred energy designated to save us from ourselves. Thus, you will fulfill a destiny of honour.

In this, however, guidance is required, to enable us choose and speak the words which will grant us divine ascent in the journey of life. This letter is written solely for this purpose. Thus, the earthman is admonished in this treatise never to speak words that will degrade his consciousness in the divine scale of existence. We are seriously warned not to speak unwanted words embedded

ANNOTATION:
Saint Paul wrote: "Let no corrupt communication proceed out of your mouth, but that which is good to the use of edifying, that it may minister grace unto the hearers" (Eph. 4:29).

in the mode of darkness. Don't just open your mouth and speak anyhow. It is better that you remain silent and listen than to speak meaningless words. 'The Grail Message' of Abd-ru-shin admonished the earthmen thus:

> ***"When a thought suddenly strikes you, keep it back, do not utter it at once, but nourish it; for it will condense through being retained in silence, and gain strength like steam under counter- pressure.***

> ***"Pressure and condensation produce the quality of a magnetic activity, in accordance with the Law that all that is stronger attracts what is weak.***

> ***"Similar thought-forms are thus attracted from all sides and retained, constantly reinforcing the***

ANNOTATION:
The words of a man are also part of the fruits by which he may be known. Be very careful with your words.

> *power of your own, your original thought, yet working in such a way that through the joining of other forms the originally produced form is refined, changes, and takes on different shapes until it comes to maturity"* (The Grail Message Vol. 1, cp.6 p.36).

A wise one in the mode of goodness should listen more and talk less. A wise man, Lucius Mestrius Plutarchos (Plutarch 14- 199 CE) of Greece, author of the 'Parallel Lives' said, that **"The mind is not a vessel to be filled but a fire to be kindled".** And for the mind to be kindled, it must give birth to words that quench the fire of wickedness in our world. Plutarch also admonished thus: **"Know how to listen, and you will profit even from those who talk badly".**

Your mouth should never talk badly. Doing so is a minus for you in the journey of life, which burden you will surely bear. In the Shariyat, scripture of the ancient Lamas of Tibet, it is written that: **"Those living in the state of selflessness will speak gently and carefully, selecting their words to give life to others".** The spiritual strength of the earthman is mostly renewed in silence, and not in vain words. You may speak many words, for as long as they give life and spiritual strength to the hearers. And in this, your spiritual strength is equally renewed.

In the Holy Bible, God Himself said: **"Keep silence before Me, O islands; and let the people renew their strength"** (Isa. 41:1; KJV). Consider the 'islands' in this regard as multitude of the earthmen who speak meaningless words in the modes of passion and darkness. Those who desire to renew divine strength within themselves and rise on the path of spiritual unfoldment, will learn to speak less, work in silence, and let their actions speak for them.

ANNOTATION:
Select your words, and speak them with the intention of giving peace of mind to others. This was the ancient admonition of the Shariyat.

The Shariyat further said in this connection:

"It is in small events, such as goodness in the daily things of life, being kind to a child, speaking softly to those who can be hurt easily, non injury to a fellow creature, and the giving of one's self to others who are without the essentials of life, that spiritual unfoldment can be found".

Blessed is the man who opens his mouth in songs of praise to his Source – The Almighty; who preaches and demonstrates the gospel of Love; who offer the prayers of Peace for all. Behold, the Spirit of the Light of God will radiate in him, and through him to others in our world. And for the spiritual armour of the Lord, towards victory in the journey and battles of life, it won't ever elude him.

ANNOTATION:
The Great Lord Jesus the Christ said: "For by thy words thou shalt be justified, and by thy words thou shalt be condemned"(Math. 12:37).

Chant the eternal glories of the Almighty in your houses, Oh earthmen; you are a creature, open your mouth and let your words chant the glories of your Creator anywhere you are. When you do this, the Spirit of the Lord will come into play. And by all means, avoid speaking unwanted and meaningless words.

Above all, God Himself said: **"Whoso offereth praise glorifieth Me: and to him that ordereth his conversation aright will I shew the salvation of God"** (Psalms 50:23; KJV). We must endeavour to order our words or conversation properly in the mode of goodness only, so as to be salvaged, individually and collectively, from the vermin of the Earth-world.

Earthmen, thus ends my treatise on **'save us from ourselves'.** A word is enough for the wise. Let the Peace of the Almighty God

ANNOTATION:
I plead that you act on the essence of this my open letter -- save us from ourselves -- especially as related to sending out daily energy of love and peace into our world.

abide with the reader of this open letter.

God bless the reader; God bless our world.

Yours in the family of humanity,

Iyke Nathan Uzorma
HARBINGER OF THE LAST COVENANT

BOOKS BY
IYKE NATHAN UZORMA

Some books by Iyke Nathan Uzorma on PDF are
available @: estore.iykenathanuzorma.org
Some hard copies are available in bookshops as well as
Amazon.
PDF versions are also available via email:
harbingeroffice@gmail.com
For further enquiries call the Secretary,
Office of the Harbinger @: +234-807-563-7746
Access the author's admonitions and powerful
expositions @: Prof. Iyke Nathan Uzorma
YouTube Channel and Facebook Page

VERSES OF ETERNAL TRUTH

By Iyke Nathan Uzorma

Some readers of the 'Verses of Eternal Truth' hold that it is one of the greatest sacred writings ever given to the children of men. The Lord Himself in His diverse manifestations, as well as Extraterrestrial Intelligences of Light (Angelic Beings) in the Heavenly realms, brought it to the physical realms of Earth via the Harbinger of the Last Covenant. It is a book of higher reality of existence, and contains hidden and forbidden truths of the ages, exposed for greater excellence of the earthmen in Light. It explains the unexplained, which includes but not limited to the hidden truth and deeper mysteries of Christ of the Second Advent.

THE SEVEN CYCLES OF FAST ASTRAL ATTACK ON MONEY AND HOW TO OVERCOME
By Lyke Nathan Uzorma

This publication exposes, for the first time on Earth, the seven cycles of astral attacks 'Psychic

Monitoring Satellite System' (PMSS) of the astral chambers of darkness. The PMSS, located in the subtle aspects of the inner Space, coordinates all attacks on money in this world. This material clearly shows how to overcome each cycle of attack. Those who have studied this treatise, especially the April 2020 updated standard version, are giving testimonies from different parts of the world, on how it has guided them to enhance their finances.

HIDDEN TRUTH OF MAN AND WOMAN
By Lyke Nathan Uzorma

In the words of Frank Fiaka of Accra, Ghana, concerning this book: "This book is very deep, more revealing and very mysterious". The 'Hidden Truth of Man and Woman' unveils the last mystery of being. It is a publication of some deep mysteries unveiled for the first on Earth. It is based on the profound spiritual teachings which the Lord and some holy Angels gave to the Harbinger of the Last Covenant, as related to the unknown aspects of man and woman. And if you have never read anybook in your life, endeavour to read this one, to know what you never knew. It is a 'must read' for all married couples and those about going into marriage.

DEEPER REALITIES OF EXISTENCE VOL.1
By Lyke Nathan Uzorma

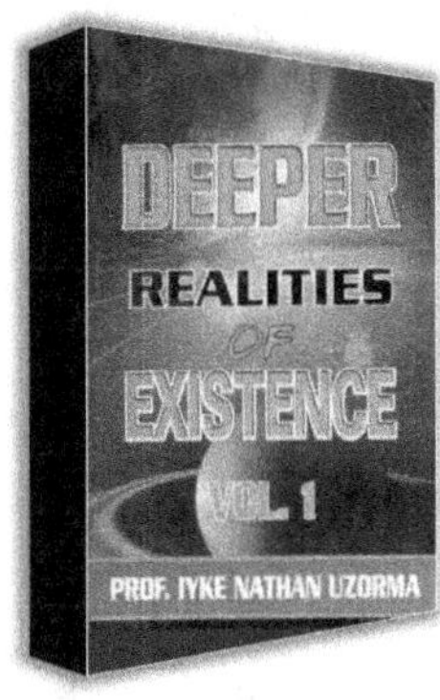

This book holds for the entire family of humanity a message of profound truth. It also brings a revelation of hidden mysteries on the practical application of Universal Divine Love. 'Deeper Realities of Existence' is provided as the panacea to all forms of physical, psychological and spiritual terrorism, including vicious astral attacks, ravaging our world. It elucidated the basis of Planetary winnowing in this age; the core terrestrial and extraterrestrial dangers of the subtle aspects of atomic radiation unknown to earthly scientists; Universal Signet of the Supreme Power of the Lord about to play out in our time; the mystery of 'mad- elephant-offence' of the forces and agents of darkness, amongst others.

SAVE US FROM OURSELVES
By Lyke Nathan Uzorma

This book provides guidance on how we can collectively defeat all that we have set in motion to destroy our world. If we put into action the admonitions of this material, we will initiate a new beginning in the formation of the 'paradise' we seek on Earth. This book also gives a strong warning to the people of this world regarding some coming calamities that will completely dwarf the COVID-19 Pandemic. It is a timely warning to a recalcitrant world.

OCCULT GRAND MASTER NOW IN CHRIST VOL. 1
By Iyke Nathan Uzorma

This publication has brought many people to the path of Christ in different parts of the world. It is the testimony of Iyke Nathan Uzorma, who rose from the peak of darkness to the Light of God. Before his direct encounter with Christ, which led to his conversion, he was the 'Living Grandmaster of the occult Order of Terrestrial and Astral Hierarchy'. Prof. Stephen Pinder Ejeh, Dean of the Faculty of Engineering of Ahmadu Bello University, Zaria, Nigeria, described this book as: "The foremost conversion testimony, renowned as the jewel of exposition of hidden powers. A book of all times on the highest game of occult deceit. It has opened the eyes of many in different parts of the world". This book shows the eternal potency of the Spirit of Christ.

OCCULT GRAND MASTER NOW IN CHRIST VOL. 2
By Iyke Nathan Uzorma

This is a powerful exposition for the liberation of man from the bondage of darkness. How the semen is used to enslave people in different ways, the manipulations of occult mirror, how diverse astral waves operate in battle against humans, how the Spirit of Christ liberates us from the yoke of subjugation, the reward of faithfulness to God, amongst other things, are contained here.

SECRETS FROM HEAVEN
By Iyke Nathan Uzorma

This book is a record of direct spiritual experience of the Harbinger of the Last Covenant with the Great Lord Jesus the Christ. The Lord visited him physically and commanded him to write down His words. The Lord then spoke to him on issues relating to the rise of man in His spiritual strength. The control of three specific centres of the body, for the excellence of the Divine Light of God in one's life, amongst other things, are well elaborated here.

MY 300 MINUTES EXPERIENCE OF HEAVEN
By Iyke Nathan Uzorma

In another occasion, the Harbinger of the Last Covenant had an intense spiritual experience wherein he was taken into the Heavenly realms of Light. There he had revelations that lasted for 300 minutes in the human terms. What are the departed saints learning now in the Heavenly realms? What are the 'Seven Duty Posts of Silence' in Heaven? How does 'The Book of Remembrance' in Heaven affect humans on Earth? What is the true meaning of 'Abraham's bosom' outside the interpretation generally given? What are the primordial elements of Universal creativity? Answers to these questions, and much more are provided in this book.

BEHOLD I GIVE UNTO YOU POWER
By Iyke Nathan Uzorma

This book is a classification of powers operating within the physical, metaphysical and spiritual systems of reality. It shows the limitations of psychic, occult and esoteric powers in approximations to the limitless Power which Christ referred to when He said: "Behold, I Give unto you Power to thread on serpents and scorpions". It is written in the light of invisible warfare, to show the Power above powers, with practical evidence and testimonies of victory.

VICIOUS OCCULT POWERS EXPOSED
By Iyke Nathan Uzorma

The book first published with the title 'Exposing the Powers of Darkness Vol. 1', is revised, enlarged and published with this title 'Vicious Occult Powers Exposed'. This publication is made solely in recognition of the highest Power embedded with the Great Lord Jesus the Christ. Here, you will learn how to be firm with the Lord, the battles that the author fought with the forces of darkness after his conversion, plus vital questions and answers, amongst others.

GREAT DIVINE IMPACT
By Iyke Nathan Uzorma

This striking treatise provides guidance for victory in the battles of life. It opens our eyes to the reality of the three stages of expression of the initial Creative Power of the Almighty God; how the third stage symbolizes our tool for conquering the network of the forces of darkness. Find out here the 'eight supreme armour', the 'seven divine principles', as well as the 'seven basic awareness' required to place one beyond the reach of the most vicious astral entities. Discover the coordinating fabrics of the realms beyond; and what is required now from above. This treatise is the revised and enlarged version of the book first published under the title 'Power for Pulling Down the Controlling Powers of Darkness'.

HIDDEN TERRORISTS
By Iyke Nathan Uzorma

The first published and the second unpublished work entitled 'How to Overcome Witches and Wizards and all the Powers of Darkness' are enlarged and published by this title: 'Hidden Terrorists'. The entire operational codes of the forces of darkness are exposed here, as well as how to completely overcome them. Apostle Dr. Moses Ayuketa of Tulsa, Oklahoma, USA, said about this book: "War is on. Let every believer read this book, to know what you never knew, of things exposed for the first time. The author, with the wealth of his experience, expounds the ground of victory for individuals, families, communities and nations". The vicious attacking army of the hosts of darkness are thoroughly exposed here.

VERSES OF GLORIOUS MARRIAGE
By Iyke Nathan Uzorma

For specific reasons revealed here, there are certain astral attacks targeted against marriages on the physical realms of Earth. There is a decree in the vicious astral chambers which goes thus: "Let there millions of marriages on Earth, but let there be no perfect agreement in love". There are two thousand minor chambers, forty main chambers and four absolute chambers in the astral realms, coordinating the battles against marriages in this world. Details of these and much more, including how to be victorious, are contained in this book. It is a revised and enlarged version of the book first published with the title 'Overcoming the Forces against Successful Marriage'.

VERSES OF WISDOM AND WATCHFULNESS
By Iyke Nathan Uzorma

The author's award winning book entitled 'Know Your Enemies Watch Your Friends' is revised, enlarged and published by this title 'Verses of Wisdom and Watchfulness'. This work simplifies how to be practically watchful of the enemy and wicked minded friends. It shows that those who ignore the path of wisdom in their dealings with people may find themselves where they least expected.

MIND RUDIMENTS Vol. 1
By Iyke Nathan Uzorma

The mind has four fundamental faculties via which the impressions of the divine Spirit, embedded with the Soul identity, pass through diverse layers of being into the physical aspects of man. When a fifth abnormal faculty is formed in the mind, it gives birth to five specific channels by which the life of a person can be dominated in the mode of ignorance. And in the mode of ignorance, the dominant mode of the multitude of people, one is enslaved. However, when the four fundamental faculties of the mind work in their normal condition, one rises in the scale of existence. Details of these are published in this book. It is an advanced divine lecture.

MIND RUDIMENTS Vol. 2
By Iyke Nathan Uzorma

'Know thyself; return to thyself and to the Light of the Almighty God', is the summary of this advanced divine lecture. This material holds that purity is the quality of the mind that makes it possible for the earthman to rise to the life of the Holy Spirit. Overall, you will understand via this material that the most important person in this world is 'you', in the light of the recognition that the prime basis of certainty is your consciousness.

THE PATH OF LIGHT Vol. 1
By Iyke Nathan Uzorma

This publication speaks much of ones divine position in the Light of God. It is the revised and enlarged version of a book initially published with the title 'The Path of Perfection Vol. 1'. If you are situated in the Light of the Consciousness of God, then every element in the Universe will, directly or indirectly, work towards the glory of the Lord in your life. Read this book to know more.

THE PATH OF LIGHT Vol. 2
By Iyke Nathan Uzorma

Every book has its author, as well as this particular book. But Iyke Nathan Uzorma strongly holds that he is not the author of this very book, though he is the channel through which it was compiled. 'The Path of Light Vol. 2' contains one of the greatest messages directly from the Lord of Creation Himself to all generations of the children of men. By special mercy, the Harbinger of the Last Covenant was brought into the radiant vicinity of the Lord of Hosts and Supreme Father of Righteousness. The divine words that he received from the Redeemer of the Oppressed' are clearly published here for the guidance of all humans. It is a must read.

DIVINE REVELATIONS Vol. 1
By Iyke Nathan Uzorma

It is written: "Surely, the Lord GOD will do nothing, but He revealeth His secret unto His servants the prophets" (Amos 3:7; KJV). 'Divine Revelations Vol. 1' contains visions and revelations of the Harbinger of the Last Covenant made for the world of man. These revelations, for different nations and our world as a whole, are related to things that will happen between 2020 to 2075 and beyond. The Lord Himself and Angelic Beings of Light are involved in all that were revealed to the author, as published here. However, there several other things revealed but yet to be published;

YOU HAVE ANOTHER YOU
By Iyke Nathan Uzorma

This is a book of deep mysteries of being. It is a guide for you to know yourself beyond your physical aspects generally known. The personality that you know as yourself, your dream bodies, your higher self, your whole self, your other 'yous' in multitudinous systems, your core multidimensional identity that gives rise to the aforementioned, amongst others, are contained in this book. This book also speaks about the purpose of being as being itself, with reasons why your spirit took the camouflage of flesh and blood in human manifestation. And much more.

TOTAL CURRENT NUMBER OF BOOKS

1. OCCULT GRAND MASTER NOW IN CHRIST VOL. 1.

2. OCCULT GRAND MASTER NOW IN CHRIST VOL. 2

3. OCCULT GRAND MASTER NOW IN CHRIST VOL. 3

4. VICIOUS OCCULT POWERS EXPOSED (Revised and Enlarged Edition of the book first published under the title 'Exposing The Rulers of Darkness Vol. 1')

5. HIERARCHY OF HIGHER MANIFESTATIONS (Revised and Enlarged Edition of the book first published under the title 'Exposing The Rulers of Darkness Vol 2')

6. THE PATH OF LIGHT VOL. 1(Revised and Enlarged Edition of the book first published under the title 'The Path of Perfection Vol. 1)

7. THE PATH OF LIGHT VOL. 2

8. THE SPIRIT REALMS VOL. 1 (A glimpse into the realms of the Forces of Light and the forces of darkness beyond the world of man: Revised and Enlarged Edition)

9. THE SPIRIT REALMS VOL. 2(More glimpse into the realms of the Forces of Light and forces of darkness beyond the world of man)

10. BEHOLD I GIVE UNTO YOU POWER

11. VERSES OF GLORIOUS MARRIAGE(Revised and Enlarged

Edition of the book first published under the title 'Overcoming The Forces Against Successful Marriage')

12. VERSES OF WISDOM AND WATCHFULNESS(Revised and Enlarged Edition of the book first published under the title 'Know Your Enemies Watch Your Friends)

13. VERSES OF ETERNAL TRUTH Hidden and forbidden truth of the ages exposed for greater excellence of the earthmen in Light

14. GREAT DIVINE IMPACT (Revised and Enlarged Edition of the book first published under the title 'Power For Pulling Down The Controlling Forces of Darkness)

15. HIDDEN TERRORISTS (Revised and Enlarged Edition of the book first published under the title 'How to Completely Overcome Witches And Wizards And All The Powers Of Darkness')

16. THE BOOK OF LIGHT

17. DEEPER REALITIES OF EXISTENCE VOL. 1

18. DEEPER REALITIES OF EXISTENCE VOL. 2

19. HIDDEN TRUTH OF MAN AND WOMAN

20. EARTHMAN RETURN TO THYSELF

21. THE KINGDOM OF GOD IS WITHIN YOU

22. INDELIBLE ENCOUNTERS

23. THE SEVEN CYCLES OF ATTACK ON MONEY AND HOW TO OVERCOME (Exposed on Earth for the first time; Revised and Enlarged Edition)

24. THE FUTURE EARTH

42. WORLDWIDE SPIRITUAL BATTLES IN NIGERIA: Before and Beyond Abacha

43. FORMER OCCULT GRAND MASTER NOW IN CHRIST SPEAKS VOL. 1

44. FORMER OCCULT GRAND MASTER NOW IN CHRIST SPEAKS VOL. 2

45. CHRIST: THE GLORIOUS MASTER

46. MIND RUDIMENTS VOL. 1

47. MIND RUDIMENTS VOL. 2

48. YOU HAVE ANOTHER YOU

49. DANGER OF SPIRITUAL COURTS

50. THE IMMUTABLE UNIVERSAL LAWS

PLUS VIDEOS, AUDIOS, MAGAZINES AND BULLETINS

NOTE: The Harbinger of the Last Covenant as at today has over 50 unpublished titles containing his media chats, messages, admonitions and public lectures.